The Circle of Life and Death

The Circle of Life and Death

✦

A Spiritual Guide for Living and Dying Well

Lawrence Karrasch, M.S.
with
Rita Karrasch, M.A.

iUniverse, Inc.
New York Bloomington

The Circle of Life and Death
A Spiritual Guide for Living and Dying Well

iUniverse books may be ordered through booksellers or by contacting:

iUniverse
1663 Liberty Drive
Bloomington, IN 47403
www.iuniverse.com
1-800-Authors (1-800-288-4677)

ISBN: 978-0-595-53152-3 (pbk)
ISBN: 978-0-595-63214-5 (ebk)

Printed in the United States of America

To God, Our Constant Companion

There is no creature which is not destined for the supreme goal,
as there is no river which is not winding its way towards the sea.
But only in the human form is consciousness so developed that it is
capable of expressing the perfection of its own true self,
which is the Self of all.

—Meher Baba

Table of Contents

Acknowledgments

Rita and I would like to acknowledge and give our heart-felt thanks to the following individuals for their loving support, guidance and assistance in bringing this book, that you now hold in your hands, to fruition.

Susan Cotler-Block
Reid Boates
Kendra Crossen-Burroughs
Charles Haynes
Sheldon Herman
Mickey Kargar
Daniel Ladinsky
Julia Ross

Introduction

Imagine planning a trip to a foreign country. The first thing you would do is consult a guidebook, describing the geography, climate, places to stay, the culture and language of the inhabitants. A well-structured guide is the key to having the most rewarding and enjoyable journey. How well you plan for this journey would determine how successful and memorable your adventure would be. If there were any cautions, you would want to know them ahead of time, to avoid unforeseen surprises. Behaving in accordance with the cultural norms would also enhance the in- depth personal interactions with the people of the country.

So, why would it be any different in planning your own life and death experiences? *The Circle of Life and Death* is designed as an introductory guide for the spiritual seeker, for planning your best life and death experience, and for answering the questions prompted from the innermost depths of your soul. What am I doing here? What is the purpose of my life? What happens to me after I die? These are just a few of the questions I have tried to answer in this book from the point of view of a seeker, who searches all the avenues in the spiritual arena to arrive at the truth. Through my spiritual searching, I have found that there are accurate answers available to us right now to live and die well.

This book draws from a broad range of esoteric and religious teachings on life, death, and rebirth from twentieth-century metaphysical writers to the prominent mystics and spiritual leaders of the modern era. I present an overview of the teachings on the soul's journey through evolution, reincarnation, and involution, along with practical strategies for living and dying well.

I was fortunate to be born into a family of spiritual seekers. Both of my parents left the traditional Catholic religion to expand their spiritual understanding of life and death issues. Therefore, I was exposed to an atmosphere in which I was encouraged to search for my individual spiritual path. Encounters with angels as a young boy was not ridiculed, but supported by my parents as well. So, it was natural for me to have an awareness of spiritual seeking at a young age. At the Rudolf Steiner School in New York City, my education was both intellectual and spiritual. In this setting, the education of the child is based on the understanding that man is a spiritual being living in a physical world. The intellect is developed without ignoring the spiritual nature of the soul.

In addition, I developed close relationships with two very important male figures, and they became my mentors throughout my life. Dr. Harry L. Kenmore, a blind chiropractor and spiritual seeker, and Meher Baba a Perfect Master living in India. Both men had profound influences on how I developed and grew as a human being with a spiritual perspective. Their impact was a guiding light for my growing up in the 1950's and 60's, a time of disillusionment and drugs. With their examples of living a purposeful life and their own intuitive spiritual attainment, I navigated through those tumultuous years with my own spiritual identity intact. To further awaken my consciousness to a spiritual way of living, I traveled to India over twenty times to engage in spiritual training.

Many people say that nothing happens by chance. In 1994, I inherited Dr. Kenmore's library of spiritual, religious, and esoteric books. It was through his study of this collection of books that Dr. Kenmore began his spiritual search. Now, I was fortunate to have this same opportunity to expand my search for a comprehensive, detailed picture of what happens to us when we die and enter the after-life.

As I said before, I was fortunate to be brought up with a belief in reincarnation, karma, and the spiritual understanding of the nature of our soul. Now, I felt a strong force propelling me to understand and assimilate the different versions of the soul's journey through life and death, and to piece together one complete picture that would encompass all the phases of our journey through this circle.

After five years of reading the works of Manly P. Hall, Max Heindel, Rudolf Steiner, Inayat Khan, C.W. Leadbeater, Annie Besant and others, I began to comprehend a certain thread of truth running through each author's conception and interpretation of this immense subject. But even with all of this material, pieces of the puzzle were still missing. So in my spare time from my career in advertising, I searched bookstores. The hunt for new and used books became my passion. Edgar Cayce, Earlyne Chaney, Dolores Cannon, Norman Vincent Peale, His Holiness The Dalai Lama and Dr. David D. Burns, to name a few, were authors my wife and I explored.

This project was becoming too big for just myself to handle, so I enlisted the help of my wife, Rita. Each summer, she devoted her time away from teaching to the project at hand. With her background in educational psychology she brought in books from Carl Jung, Eric Erickson, Howard Gardner, Daniel Goleman and others to provide a well-rounded picture of the nature of the soul's journey in life, and what happens to us when we die.

We also found that during this time the material we were researching was helping us to work out many problems we were grappling with in our own lives. Questions related to reincarnation, karma, the destiny of each soul, happiness, suffering, and the different types of death that can be experienced, along with other theme-related topics, were being answered through our research. We began to realize that we were also helping our friends and family with insights into areas that their own religious or non-religious beliefs were unable to do. I think this was the time when we decided to share this comprehensive information about life, death, and the awakening of intuition guiding one's spiritual search.

Here are just a few of the spiritual truths that we found to be a constant in the spiritual writings included in *The Circle of Life and Death*.

- It is love in one form or another that is the binding attraction that propels creation forward in the progression of the soul through life and death.

- The continuation of the consciousness of our soul is assured through the circle of life and death.

- Life and death should be viewed not as two separate experiences but as one continuous progression repeated over and over.

- Our karma in each life is a result of our actions from our past lives and our present behavior. Our actions in our present life will also impact and create our future and affect how we experience the after-life.

- Our purpose in life is to gain experiences that will lead us to a higher consciousness, the spark of God within us. This is the driving force that propels each individual soul through the cycle of reincarnation.

- The purpose of death is an opportunity to end the cycle of births and deaths by uniting with the Clear Light, God. Until the Final Death, we are given the opportunity in the after-life, to refine and assimilate the experiences we had on earth, so we may incorporate this wisdom into our ever-growing higher consciousness.

The Indian Sanskrit word, sanskaras (impressions) is presented in a new light as the DNA of karma in the reincarnation process. Other books have talked about the immortality of the soul. *The Circle of Life and Death* goes a step further in describing how the soul can continue to progress through each life, with the ego-mind providing the continuity between lives, keeping its own set of Akashic Records recorded as impressions or sanskaras.

This book is structured from the seeker's point of view as a guide for living and dying well. Each chapter is designed to be concise and understandable for applying the principles and information in our modern lives. We live in a world of uncertainty, where our life and those of our loved ones may tragically end during a routine day. There is a way to live our life in these times to be happy and yet prepare for a death that may come sooner than we expect.

At the end of each chapter, I have included a section called *Chapter Reflections to Guide Your Spiritual Search*. These bullet points are aimed at reiterating key concepts for reflection by the reader to enhance the experience with each chapter. Practical strategies are also incorporated into this section to prepare you for your best life-and-death experience.

Part One: *"The Advancing Stream of Life,"* provides an explanation of how every individual soul unconsciously originates from God to begin the progression of life and death. Each life's purpose brings us one step closer to consciously reunite with God, our final goal, through the continuous cycle of reincarnation. Death, as the counterpart of life's experiences, provides our soul and our spirit bodies a time to subjectively assimilate and modify our consciousness to prepare us to return to earth with a greater wealth of intuitive wisdom.

Part Two: *"The Influence of Universal Laws"* introduces the unbiased principles that operate throughout every aspect of creation. This section reveals how our life unfolds with karmic patterns of memory through successive incarnations. Remembering our past lives in detail would only complicate how we experience our lessons in each incarnation on earth while we learn how to connect intuitively with our higher self.

Part Three: *"The Development of Consciousness,"* explains how our consciousness progresses and unfolds through each life by the concept of sanskaras (impressions): the DNA of karma. Recognizing our own thoughts and intuition from the floating outside thoughts of others combined with discipline of the mind will assure us the happiness we deserve and avoid unnecessary suffering. We are given a period of reprieve from our burden of karmic impressions during sleep to temporarily, unconsciously reunite with God.

Part Four: *"Understanding Death from a Spiritual Perspective"* focuses on the nature of death, preparing for the *"Clear Light of the Void"*, God, at the moment of death and the soul's after-life experiences. Understanding death from a spiritual perspective allows us to enter this transitional phase unencumbered with traditional fears and apprehension.

Part Five: *"The Propelling Force of Love in the Circle of Life and Death"* completes the soul's journey in the after-life to once again prepare for the next incarnation on earth. As we plan for our new incarnation, we look ahead to joining our loved ones and soulmates in a new life. Until our soul is consciously reunited with the Oversoul, God, we can be assured that our immortal soul will spend lifetime after lifetime with those we love.

I hope this book will guide you to consciously begin to embark on a life-changing experience. This is an individual inner journey that my wife and I continue to share with all spiritual seekers. All religions and philosophies are linked together like beads on one string with the goal accessible to everyone through whichever path you choose to travel. Just keep an open mind and heart. The best life-and-death experience awaits you on your journey.

"Oh, heart, if the ignorant say to you that the soul perishes like the body, answer that the flower perishes, but the seeds remain. This is the law of God.[1]*"*

Larry Karrasch
Rita Karrasch
Myrtle Beach, SC

1. Gibran, Kahlil. *The Kahlil Gibran Reader,* 29

PART I
The Advancing Stream of Life

1

The Progression of the Soul Through Life and Death

○ ○

"The soul, ultimately disappointed in human relationships, must turn from its attachments to outward forms, and bestow its affections upon those imperishable truths which alone can satisfy man's yearnings."

—Manly P. Hall *

The search for meaning in life and what happens to you in death is defined by the religious teachings and traditions that you believe and practice. When you grow up in an atmosphere of a particular religion, that belief system is perceived as the truth and you base your understanding of life and death upon its foundation. This belief system instilled by your parents, which was instilled by their parents, is accepted with no questions asked—without proof. But at some point, you may begin to sense that your questions about life and death are not being answered through your religious beliefs alone. Yet, it is extremely difficult to go beyond what has been instilled in you as a child, especially behaviors related to God and religion.

Your search may begin when a personal crisis impacts your life and suddenly the foundation of your belief system is undermined. You may now be ready to open your heart and mind to find the answers to the questions arising from the very depth of your being. Where do I go from here? Does my consciousness die with my physical form? Will my personality survive? Is there another form of existence after I die? Do my actions in life affect my existence after death? This is the inner struggle for each soul, seeking the answers that may lie beyond the capacity of their religion.

When the messiahs and prophets periodically unveil the meaning of life and death, they do so according to the intellectual level and culture of humanity for that time. But throughout history, Eastern and Western religious ideologies associated with each particular prophet or messiah is written after their demise. The essence of their teachings, passed on through the centuries, eventually becomes diluted and even adulterated so that a true picture of what happens to the individual soul after death is still hidden behind the veil of religious dogmas.1

> When we study the religions given by various prophets to different people in this world in different periods of the world's history, we shall find that the truth which is behind all the religions is the same; if the teachings differs it differs only in the law they have given. People have always disputed in vain over the difference in the laws that the different teachers have given to their people, not realizing how much that law depended on the people who received it and on the time when it was given.2

When your heart and mind are opened to new perspectives about the progression of the soul through life and death, the principle of reincarnation may have a certain ring of truth. Reincarnation is one of the oldest beliefs in recorded religious history.3 Rebirth teaches that each individual soul is a part of God's unconscious Being. The individual soul reincarnates in human form through countless lifetimes in the physical world to experience all the earthly opposites of life until the ego consciousness is worn down. Eventually, consciousness slowly turns inward (involution) to reveal the true nature of our very being. Then we can end the circle of birth and death.4

If you could access the memories from your past incarnations, you would actually find that you have lived before as a Christian, Hebrew, Moslem, Buddhist, or even an atheist.5 By getting in touch with your spiritual self (which is that unconscious spark of God within), you will have a chance to rediscover the oneness and unity of all religions and the acceptance of reincarnation.

Without the concept of reincarnation, each newly created soul sent from God would only spend one short life in the physical world on earth: rich or poor, healthy or sick, intelligent or ignorant, with no rhyme or reason for how and why life unfolds. As the soul passes into death, this soul would be judged for this one life led. The thoughts and actions of the just-completed life would then determine whether this soul would remain in heaven or hell for all eternity.

In the Divine scheme of Creation why some lives are benefited: by health, mental balance, loving families, and material wealth and others have the misfortune of sickness, mental dysfunction, abusive lives, poverty, and tragedy cannot be answered. Even the question of why people are born male or female, die at birth or live to the age of ninety, or die a natural or unnatural death cannot be answered without rebirth. Without reincarnation, we cannot understand the true nature of our soul and why we live and die. At one time, even the Christian doctrines referred to rebirth in their teachings of the early Bible. But through the centuries, Christianity has narrowed the scope of their doctrines to almost eliminate rebirth entirely.6 The hierarchy justified this simplification of the teachings as a means to provide order and stability to the believers during a time of intellectual darkness. With one life to live, the way to God was only possible through Jesus Christ and the church hierarchy as the intermediaries.7

The Advancing Stream of Life is a philosophy that encompasses and incorporates the concepts from all the great religious teachings in their original essence.8 This belief system has been instrumental in guiding my life as a spiritual seeker. It is a culmination of ancient teachings brought forth for humanity in this new age of intuitive understanding. The nature of our soul is shown to be emerging from God as an individualized soul, as an unconscious bubble in God's Divine Ocean. The goal and purpose for each of us as this *"unconscious bubble"* is to journey through evolution, reincarnation and involution—as described by Meher Baba—to arrive at the answer to the question: Who am I? At the end of our journey the answer manifests, I come from God, therefore I Am God. This is our divine inner unfoldment.

Darwin's theory of evolution stated that natural selection and random mutation was the driving force that created physical forms. The progression of life and death is actually driven by our individual soul's developing conscious need for certain types of experiences. Therefore, we assume physical forms during evolution and reincarnation to meet the needs of our developing consciousness.9 Our consciousness does not develop from the physical form as in the Darwinian theory. Form, therefore, follows the function of our developing consciousness and the need for certain experiences.10

Our soul begins the evolutionary journey through the lower kingdoms. As we experience our first human form, reincarnation begins. Through life experiences and the assimilation of these experiences at death, in the after-life, our soul's consciousness is slowly awakened to eventually know itself consciously as a part of God. Through the process of involution (the last stage of our soul's journey), we yearn to be reunited with the Divine Creator.

As we begin to go beyond our religious teachings and practices to search for the answers to the riddle of life and death, a divine inner unfoldment will begin. You do not need to abandon all your religious beliefs to embark on this journey.

Huston Smith said, *"If we take the world's enduring religions at their best, we discover the distilled wisdom of the human race."*11 If you merely follow all the rituals and ceremonies of your family's religion, without tapping into your spiritual intuition, your purpose in life will not be fulfilled. As Huston Smith said, take the best of each religion. This will bring you closer to your true relationship with the Divine Essence and the purpose of your life and death.

Chapter Reflections to Guide Your Spiritual Search

- You do not have to abandon all your current beliefs to open your heart and mind to a new spiritual approach.

- There are as many paths to God as there are individual souls in creation.

- Each individual soul needs to find his or her own spiritual path.

- Reincarnation is one of the oldest beliefs in recorded history.

- Quietude is the first step to find the divine within.

- Develop your inner faculties, through prayer, meditation, silence, and reading inspirational books. This will guide you to get in touch with your intuitive self.

References

1. Hall, Manly P. *Questions and Answers*, 60-61, 68-75
2. Khan, Inayat. *Mastery Through Accomplishment*, 59
3. Hinduism and Buddhism both incorporate reincarnation in there teachings.
4. Heindel, Max. *The Rosicrucian Christianity Lectures*, vol.11, 9-25
5. Todeschi, Kevin J. *Edgar Cayce on the Akashic Records*, 168
6. Langley, Noel. *Edgar Cayce on Reincarnation*, 169-178, 179-201
7. Duce, Ivy O. *What Am I Doing Here?*, 23-27
8. Baba, Meher. *Discourses*, 339
9. Hall, Manly P. *Death To Rebirth*, 35-37
10. Baba, Meher. *The Advancing Stream of Life*, 22-27, 31
11. Smith, Huston. *The Wisdom of Faith with Huston Smith*, PBS interview

   *Hall, Manly P. *Questions and Answers*, 4

2

The Purpose of Life

o o o o o o o o o o o o o o o o o o o o o o o o

"Life is an ongoing adventure of purposeful experiences and relationships, enabling individuals to find their true selves. Deep within each soul there is an impelling force guiding that individual to discover who am I? In essence, we are all seekers, seeking our true identity and our relationship to the Whole."

—*Kevin J. Todeschi* *

" *'What is the meaning of it, Watson?' said Holmes solemnly as he laid down the paper. "What object is served by this circle of misery and violence and fear? It must tend to some end, or else our universe is ruled by chance, which is unthinkable. But what end? There is the great standing perennial problem to which human reason is as far from the answer as ever.' "*1 Sir Arthur Conan Doyle in his story, *The Cardboard Box,* has Sherlock Holmes questioning his purpose in life. Being the great detective that he is he admits intellectual reasoning will not provide the answer.

Inayat Khan, a Sufi master, explains that every individual soul returns to earth lifetime after lifetime with a definite purpose or goal. With each lifetime, your consciousness makes advances towards awakening your inner self to find its true reality. Each life is important for your advancement towards this goal. In later chapters, I will discuss how your soul decides with your guardian angel prior to birth the right time period, the country, race, family, religion, a male or female form, and which karmic debts should be worked out for that lifetime. For now, it is important to understand how you can recognize what your purpose may be in your current life.

Throughout human existence, consciousness developed from instinct to reason. Humanity's current stage of consciousness, due in part to the process of reincarnation, is advancing from reason to intuition.2 As we enter this age, intuition is available for us to tap into and discover our main goal in life and ultimately find our true reality.

Inayat Khan identifies our real intuition as that which is found in the *"depths of one's being."* When you become one-pointed in awakening your intuition, it will become more readily and easily accessible in your daily life. Once this occurs, it then becomes necessary to believe and trust in this intuition so that you may act accordingly. Do not try to reason with the mind what your heart knows and feels intuitively. *"What you understand by intuition is always true. What you understand by intellect is sometimes true and sometimes not."*3

With intuition as a tool, you can search for clues leading to your purpose through a method similar to detective work. Uncovering such clues as your latent talents, abilities, interests, physical attributes, and family conditions while quieting your mind, will give you the intuition to bring forth insights that can lead you to identify and understand your true purpose for this life.

Your career purpose in this life might not always be the most obvious road to take. Your family might be guiding you to pursue a career that you are not intuitively drawn to. Instead, your path may lead you to discover and develop a hidden talent in music, art, science, or humanitarian pursuits. With the discovery of your life's work, you should have a feeling of joy, renewed energy, and a sense of God's presence as this path unfolds.

Once you begin this process of discovering your true purpose, at whatever stage of life you find yourself, you can then choose a path to lead you there. You may need to get the education and experiences that will provide the unfolding of your talents and abilities for the career or special work ahead in this life. You most probably will be picking up in this life where you left off in your last incarnation.4 Your life's purpose cannot always be achieved in one lifetime. You, therefore, begin your purpose from where you are now.

A remembrance of the spiritual perspective as the *"bigger picture"* is most important when searching for your life's work. Whether you are embarking on your first experience as an adult or as a retiree, you can get in tune with what you need to be doing in life at this time. Because the advancing stream of life is a continuous circle of births and deaths it is never too late to develop any aspect of your purpose in life.

The accumulated strengths and weaknesses from past lives are what you have to work with in this life. Manly P. Hall, a twentieth century philosopher, tells us that:

> *In this life we refine a little more the fabric of ourselves. Having learned a few more lessons, having found a little more truth, having done a little more of good, having come a little closer to perfection, we call this life finished, depart for a little time, and then return to continue the task of searching for the Real.5*

In addition to your life's career, there are many interwoven challenges you are expected to experience and overcome. If you understand that challenges help your consciousness develop and awaken, you will not be afraid when they enter your life. When you face each challenge, you are overcoming a weakness that will bring you closer to your higher nature.6 You do not face challenges alone. God as your *"constant companion"* is always providing guidance as your silent partner. At the present time your consciousness may not be attuned to acknowledge this companionship. If you pray to God with all your heart and not your mind, God will become your *"constant companion"*. Epictetus said, *"Think of God more than you breathe."* Then your remembrance of God will be constant, especially at the moment of death.

Each lifetime presents a specific set of problems to work through and a chance to develop new strengths to face your next challenge. So, during each lifetime, whatever you choose to learn, experience, improve, and progress in, you need to keep in your mind's eye that this is but one chapter in your individual book of life.

Chapter Reflection to Guide Your Spiritual Search

- Every individual soul returns to earth lifetime after lifetime with a definite purpose or goal.

- When you feel intuitively prompted, a feeling of joy, renewed energy, and a sense of God's presence will unfold.

- If something is meant to be to enhance your life's purpose, *"it will happen."* One should hold fast to an intuitive decision through the ups and downs and carry it to a logical end. Do not waiver but also be flexible because spiritual development is not a rigid process.

- Remember in life there is a multitude of purposes simultaneously advancing you to your goal. These purposes are sometimes all intertwined with one another. For example, relationships between husbands and wives, parents and children, brothers and sisters, workers and business partners do not occur in isolation from each other.

- *"God's purpose is that we make ourselves a channel through which His spirit may manifest."*[7]

Reference

1.   Doyle, Sir Arthur Conan. *The Complete Novel and Stories.* vol. 11, 378
2.   Baba, Meher. *Meher Baba on Inner Life*, 65
3.   Kachuri, Bhau. *Lord Meher*, 2618
4.   Todeschi, Kevin J. *Edgar Cayce on the Akashic Records*, 124
5.   Hall, Manly P. *Questions and Answers*, 15
6.   Todeschi, Kevin J. *Edgar Cayce on the Akashic Records*, 72
7.   Cayce, Edgar. www.are-cayce.com. *Oneness.*

   *Todeschi, Kevin J. *Edgar Cayce on the Akashic Records*, 173

3

The Purpose of Death

o o o o o o o o o o o o o o o o o o o o o o o

"The soul is life, it never touches death. Death is its illusion, its impression; death comes to something the soul holds, not to the soul itself."

—*Inayat Khan* *

Every one of us will eventually experience death at the end of each lifetime. What is the purpose of death? The main purpose of the death experience, from the spiritual perspective, provides every individual soul the opportunity to be freed from the circle of life and death—liberation.1 Although we have this opportunity, we usually miss this moment at death, because our mind is preoccupied with the life we are leaving behind. Therefore, during life, we need to train our consciousness to be ready for this opportunity of liberation.

As a child on a merry-go-round, the focus is on capturing the golden ring with each revolution. Our prize in the circle of life and death is capturing the *"pearl of great price."* This pearl is the luminous light of God who greets us at the moment of death. This light is known as the *"First Clear Light of the Void."* 2 At the moment of death, most of us are too preoccupied with preconceived fears of death, thoughts of leaving our loved ones, and material possessions. When this radiant light approaches us, we miss it. We have not prepared our

11

consciousness to focus our attention so completely at the time of death to embrace our true goal—this chance for liberation.

Spiritual teachers remind their students to keep God as their *"constant companion."* By doing this they can develop the habit of heartfelt thinking of God several times a day. Then, at the moment of death they will automatically turn their attention to *"The Light,"* God. Take heart, most people miss this chance! But through the process of reincarnation, God gives each individual soul the opportunity once again to prepare for this meeting at the end of each lifetime spent on earth. Eventually, after many lifetimes, each individual soul will be successful; for this is the true purpose of death.

So, what will be the purpose of death if the Clear Light of Liberation is missed? At this moment, the soul now enters the vastness of the invisible world, the after-life, and has a chance to glimpse and experience the true nature of the immortality of the soul. Each of us, as an immortal individual soul, continues our spiritual advancement, beginning with our life panorama review. We then spend a subjective existence in the Heaven-or Hell-state to assimilate all our thoughts, feelings, and actions from the just-finished life. The purpose of this is to modify our soul's consciousness so that when we return to earth in our next incarnation, our ego-mind will have unveiled within it's being a greater wealth of intuitive wisdom.3

> *During the period of its physical life the personality absorbs into itself certain knowledge and experience. After death this knowledge is transferred to the higher parts of the personality; that is, the mind and the emotions.... The substance or essence of experience, refined by karma, then becomes part of the permanent entity, and the personality has completed its purpose of existence.4*

To most individuals, death is the greatest tragedy of life. But to those who recognize the flip-flop of life and death, each individual soul is in its true element after death without the cumbersome physical form.

> *Death is the spirit casting off the bonds of flesh, to function for a time in the invisible world before building another vehicle of physical manifestation. Thus while death seems to the uninformed to be a great tragedy, it is understood by the philosopher as a magnificent spiritual experience, life's supreme adventure—the return of the spirit to its own state, and a release of inner greatness from bondage to the limitations of inadequate flesh.5*

To experience the physical world, your individual soul puts on a covering called the physical form. Your body and the five senses become the medium for your soul to express itself in the physical world. Let us imagine, as the spiritual teachings portray, that each lifetime is like a man who puts on and takes off a suit of clothes. Another conceptual image is that of an astronaut who must cover his body with an awkward space suit in order to be able to survive a space walk. He is limited in all of his actions by the suit. This is uncomfortable but most necessary for his survival and experiences in outer space.

Many people actually yearn for death and the discarding of the uncomfortable suit of clothes when their problems in life become overwhelming. Unfortunately, death is not an ending of problems. Problems are a necessary challenge that you come to the earth to solve and overcome. An aspect of your life's purpose is to awaken your spiritual intuition to understand that problems help your consciousness develop. It is for this expansion of your consciousness that you must live and face your challenges. Each of us receives the guidance, unveiled from our inner resources as the need arises, to face each challenge.6 As we review our experiences in the after-life, we will know that we actually reap the benefits of overcoming the very obstacles that caused such frustration in life.

When death finally comes, as it does for everyone, it should be faced with an inner conviction that I have done this many times before. But how does one awaken to this conviction? Most of us do not have a clear memory of ever having passed through death's portal. Belief that there is something beyond the visible world is a first step in awakening this inner conviction. A trust in the individuals who experience and reveal the true nature of death can come when you open your mind and heart to this unseen world. Reading the written works of seers and advanced souls with an open mind is a second step. Mystical teachings from the major religions and esoteric philosophies contain stories written in allegories and literal accounts of the after-life. As we have experienced all this before, it should ring true in the very depths of our being. Discussions with other seekers in the search for truth will also shake off the cobwebs of our instilled childhood conceptions and fears about death.

Once awakened to the purpose of death, learning about the process of death and preparing for it should take on a new meaning for you. Since death could come to you and your loved ones at any time, you need to realize that you have no time to lose in this preparation. To have the best after-death experience takes a lifetime of preparation. Every thought, word, feeling, and action in life will define your experience in the after-life. How you lived on earth creates the record for how you will exist in the after-life, which we call death.

Benjamin Franklin wrote his own epitaph to be placed upon his gravestone, demonstrating an understanding that death is a refining process to bring out the best qualities of the individual soul for the next life.

The body of Benjamin Franklin
(Like the cover of an old book,
Its contents torn out,
And stript of its lettering and guilding),
Lies here food for worms;
Yet the work itself shall not be lost,
For it will appear once more
In a new and more beautiful edition
Corrected and amended
By The Author 7

Chapter Reflections to Guide Your Spiritual Search

- Prepare yourself for *"The Clear Light of the Void,"* God, at the moment of death. Train your consciousness during life, to be ready for this opportunity of liberation.

- Be assured that your consciousness will continue throughout your soul's journey. The spiritual bodies are not less by dying.

- Learn to repeat a name of God automatically, so that in times of crisis you will not forget to call out to Him.

- Pray to God, the Universal Oversoul, as death grows near.

- How you lived on earth creates the record for how you will exist in the after-life, which we call death.

References

1. Sambhava, Padma. *The Tibetan book of the Dead.* Translated by Robert A.F. Thurman, 45-50
2. Chaney, Earlyne. *The Mystery of Death and Dying,* 43-69
3. Hall, Manly P. *Reincarnation: The Cycle of Necessity,* 155-163
4. Hall, Manly P. *Reincarnation: The Cycle of Necessity,* 158
5. Hall, Manly P. *Questions and Answers,* 89
6. Khan, Inayat. *Mastery Through Accomplishment,* 65-68
7. Hall, Manly P. *Death to Rebirth,* 16

   *Khan, Inayat. *The Sufi Message of Hazrat Inayat Khan,* 165-166

4

The Soul and the Spirit Bodies

o o o o o o o o o o o o o o o o o o o o o o o o o

"Immortality of the individualized soul is made possible by the fact that the individualized soul is not the same as the physical body. The individualized soul continues to exist with all its sanskaras in the inner worlds through its mental and subtle bodies, even after it has discarded its gross body at the time of death."

—*Meher Baba* *

If you believe in one life, you probably think of yourself as a human being with a physical body and a soul. In esoteric teachings, there is more to us then meets the eye. By understanding the nature of the soul and the progression from life to death through reincarnation, we learn that we actually consist of a total of four different bodies (including our physical form) while we live on earth. *"Man has four bodies, of which the physical is the lowest and most dense. When he casts off the mortal coil, he merely transfers his consciousness to his finer vehicles, which he continues to use in the invisible worlds."*1

In her book, *What Am I Doing Here?*, Ivy O. Duce describes the relationship of the physical body to the different spiritual bodies that make up the totality of the human being. Ivy O. Duce uses the egg to represent the soul's four bodies.

Starting with the outer shell as the gross or physical body of the human being, we progress inwardly to the membrane designated as the etheric shell. The subtle and mental bodies correspond to the white and yolk respectively.2

As you live on earth, your individual soul will experience life and death through the four bodies functioning in unison, each composed of material related to its own nature. Your physical body that is visible to the five senses is the most dense and composed of matter in the form of solids, liquids, and gaseous states. Your etheric body is made up of the ethers, not visible to the normal eye, allowing your life force or prana to interpenetrate your physical form. Your subtle/emotional body is the giver of this energy life force sustaining your physical existence. Desires and emotions emanate through the subtle body. In the analogy of the egg, the yolk or mental body holds the mind and all the faculties of your thinking. Both are composed of a finer vibrational matter.

When you go to sleep, your subtle and mental bodies can withdraw to leave your etheric and physical bodies behind. While they remain attached by the silver cord, this separation actually allows your etheric body to perform functional repairs and revitalize the physical form. Through this attachment, your subtle and mental bodies can return to your sleeping form when you wake up. However, at the time of your death, when your individual soul has completed its sojourn in this life, the silver cord will be severed. This allows your physical body to die. Then, within three to four days, the etheric, subtle, and mental bodies will detach from your earthly form permanently.3

At the time of your conception, the etheric shell acts as an intermediary, forming the matrix for the development of your physical, subtle, and mental bodies in your mother's womb. Your physical form grows, according to this matrix pattern, using nutrients and matter from your mother.4 Also, your etheric shell is responsible for the later development of your astral form that will contain your subtle and mental bodies as they depart at the time of your death into the invisible world.5

When you are born into the world, the etheric shell always remains attached to your physical body, even during sleep. Then, at death, this shell remains close to your physical form. This is the "ghost" that clairvoyants can see at the grave. It will slowly deteriorate at the same rate that the physical form decomposes. If your physical form has been embalmed, the etheric shell will last longer. If your body is cremated, the etheric shell is immediately destroyed. This etheric ghost maintains all of the thought forms that you once possessed. But it is not capable of its own individual thoughts or free will.6

The white of the egg, as described by Ivy O. Duce, is your subtle body extending several inches beyond the physical form. This extension is called your aura of energy. In physical terms, this is also called your "personal space", as described by Edward T. Hall in his book, *The Hidden Dimension*. If a person entering your personal space is not in tune with your vibrational level, you will begin to feel uncomfortable. It is a mixing of auras of conflicting vibrations which causes this discomfort.7

The interesting aspect of how your physical body can function, grow, and use energy is that all of the four soul bodies act in unison, deriving energy or chi through the subtle/emotional body which is the powerhouse of the life force (Prana). To further understand this concept, think of the Sun as God as was done in ancient times. Then, the subtle body can be envisioned as a solar cell that converts the Sun's (God's) energy into electricity to run the motors (organs) of the physical body.

Let us take this understanding of the function of the subtle body one step further. The desires and emotions we experience in each incarnation are expressed through the emotional seed atom located approximately in the area of the solar plexus of your physical body. This emotional seed atom stores a record of your emotional character to be developed by your individual soul—its strengths and weaknesses. This includes all of your emotions and desires for this lifetime. It provides the range of possible personality traits for your soul to fulfill its purpose in life. Through free will, we can manipulate these traits within the range of possibilities.8

Now, let us say that Peter is born into an alcoholic family and, as he grows up, he shows alcoholic tendencies. Most people would say that he inherited these personality weaknesses from his alcoholic father. From the spiritual perspective, we can understand that these tendencies may not physically manifest strictly through the concept of genetics. They may originate from Peter's own store of weaknesses in his emotional seed atom. Not every child born into this family will exhibit alcoholic tendencies. Cravings for alcohol are not given to the soul by the father; they are the individual soul's own impressions which he brings with him to this life housed in this emotional seed atom.

The spiritual interpretation is that Peter chose his parents because of the karma that he needs to work out in dealing with his alcoholic problem. His genetic make-up will need to have DNA that will impair alcohol metabolism and create the addiction tendency. So Peter needs parents who are able to pass on this genetic combination for his addiction to occur through his physical body. Peter will need to overcome this karmic obstacle of alcohol addiction until he is successful. This challenge may be part of his overall life's purpose. In each lifetime, a soul is given a chance to complete a specific karmic action.9

The last part of our egg analogy is the mental body, represented by the yolk. All of the soul's potential range of thoughts to be accessed in this lifetime is contained in the mental seed atom positioned in the pineal gland of the brain.10 The mental body has two divisions, a lower and higher level. The lower level of the mind, the intellectual faculties, is undeveloped spiritually. Animal passions and concrete thinking are prevalent. When the higher mental body is developed less instinctual behavior is observed. At this stage, the individual has gained mental abilities that are more in tune with abstract reasoning and loftier spiritual aspirations.11 It is, therefore, in our best spiritual interest to cultivate the higher sphere of our mental body.

Theosophy teaches us—that through art, music, the appreciation of beauty in nature, and other creative pursuits—we can develop this higher mental level. Outside thoughts will always pass through one's mind influencing the direction of one's mental growth. As we develop the higher faculties of mind we should be constantly guiding the intellect to function as a vehicle of its own free will—linked to God's will. In this way, we will be in a better position to achieve our spiritual purpose and strengthen our spirit. The mental and subtle bodies (mind and energy) are the spirit of the soul.12

Shati Gwain and Norman Vincent Peale suggest it is always wise to have loving positive thoughts, especially at the time of death. So, during your life, you can experience positive thoughts and actions and develop a habit that will automatically draw positive thoughts to you in the after-life. Positive thoughts will be creating positive actions, which in turn will perpetuate more positive energy. This creates a cycle whereby the Universal Laws of Attraction and Like Begets Like, explored in the next chapter, function to elevate the vibrational level of all your soul bodies.

Finally, in order for our four bodies to function as a whole unit, the ego came into being. The ego is the center of consciousness, positioned in the mental body, sometimes referred to as the ego-mind. This ego allows our individual soul to intelligently regulate all the impressions *("accumulated imprints of past experiences, which determine one's desires and actions")*13 contained in our seed atoms. Without the ego, the psychic energy contained in the mental body would be frittered away and dissipated if the ego as a nucleus did not take stock of all acquired positive and negative desires, thoughts, and emotions. As Meher Baba describes: *"The formation of the ego serves the purpose of giving a certain amount of stability to conscious processes and also serves as a working equilibrium, which makes for a planned and organized life."*14

Here is a closing depiction of how the spiritual bodies work through our physical form. A thought is formed in the mental body. Then our subtle body converts this thought to energy, giving it emotion and desire for us to carry out the original thought. Through the process of free will, the thought and desire will manifest in the form of an action visible to all, in the physical world we call earth.

This chapter provided an overview for understanding the nature of the four bodies of our soul and how they are interdependent and interwoven, allowing us to function, gain, and assimilate experiences in life and death. We can now proceed to discuss the Universal Laws operating and affecting us as multidimensional spiritual and physical beings.

Chapter Reflections to Guide Your Spiritual Search

- While we live on earth, we are actually multi-bodied individuals, consisting of a physical form and three spirit bodies. At death, we shed our physical form.

- The invisible bodies of man are discernable to spiritually advanced souls and clairvoyants.

- Knowing that we are more than a physical being, we can choose to use our higher mental faculties to guide our thoughts and actions.

- When we exercise moderation and control in all aspects of living, our physical body will not rule our emotions and mind.

- Positive thinking can only draw and produce positive results.

- Faith, love, sharing, forgiveness and compassion will help build a refined emotional body.

- Associate with inspirational ideas and people to raise the levels of your subtle and mental bodies.

References

1. Hall, Manly P. *Death To Rebirth,* 11
2. Duce, Ivy O. *What Am I Doing Here?,* 35
3. Chaney, Earlyne, *The Mystery of Death and Dying,* 54-59, 63, 96
4. Heindel, Max. *The Rosicrucian Cosmo-Conception,* 137-141
5. Chaney, Earlyne, *The Mystery of Death and Dying,* 59-61
6. Leadbeater, C.W. *The Astral Plane,* 71-74
7. Hall, Manly P. *Questions and Answers,* 30-31
8. Chaney, Earlyne, *The Mystery of Death and Dying,* 13-18
9. Chaney, Earlyne, *The Mystery of Death and Dying,* 15
10. Chaney, Earlyne, *The Mystery of Death and Dying,* 19-20
11. Hall, Manly P. *Questions and Answers,* 40-44
12. Baba, Meher. *Discourses,* 16-22
13. Baba, Meher, *Discourses,* 417
14. Baba, Meher. *Discourses,* 161

    * Baba, Meher. *Discourses,* 304

PART 2
The Influence of Universal Laws

5

The Universal Laws in the Circle of Life and Death

○ ○

"Life in the earth was designed to be an orderly growing experience. The physical realm was imagined as a dimension with very special qualities, in a universe of dimensions. The entire realm and all it contains are held in place by forces we call universal laws. Our lives here and, in fact, time and space would not exist without them. Fortunately, universal laws are unchangeable, even though we often wish they were not.

—*Harvey A. Green* *

The evolutionary process is constantly advancing forward in an orderly fashion, with all of creation in the physical and spiritual worlds held in place by forces called Universal Laws. The laws originate from God, not from humanity. They are not prejudicial as they work equally for humanity and all of the lower kingdoms in creation. The Universal Laws shape and maintain materiality and spirituality. Without these laws, the universe would not progress forward in evolution and reincarnation in an orderly manner—chaos would reign.

Included in this chapter are the Universal Laws, which have a major influence on the soul's journey through life and death. The laws presented, based on Edgar Cayce's psychic discourses from the book, *Your Life: Why It Is the Way It Is and What You Can Do About It*, by Bruce MacArthur, should provide a clear understanding of each law's influence in the material and spiritual realms.

Like Begets Like

We can view the Law of Like Begets Like as we work to achieve our life's purpose. You first need to build harmony and peace within yourself if you are seeking to create harmonious relationships. At this level, you can attract other individual souls into your sphere or circle of friends that are now like yourself because you have first created harmony from within. Nothing harmonious could be an outcome of chaos. The vibrational level at which your emotional or subtle body is resonating calls forth and blends with other individuals of similar vibrational levels. A person with a violent nature attracts violence and discord, while an individual with a gentle nature gathers fellow spirits engaged in compassionate activities. The whole environment you live in, therefore, has the element of what you bring and develop in each lifetime.

Like Begets Like is the law in which freedom of choice plays an active role. Your spiritual nature develops through this freedom of choice. Once you begin to move in a spiritual direction, you will begin to notice a change in your inner perspective towards yourself and others. Changing your attitude and accepting the God within, as your guide and *"constant companion,"* draws into your life what you need to achieve for your life's purpose. All that is needed is patience, trust, and faith.

Law of Attraction

Once you begin to cultivate an inner life of peace, joy, and harmony by changing your attitude and balancing your emotions, the Law of Attraction will draw people and situations into your life that will help your spiritual development. The Law of Like Begets Like and the Law of Attraction work together through an energy level called our aura. Our aura surrounds our physical body. As Edgar Cayce describes in his readings, *"Apparently the aura reflects the vibrations of the soul."*[1]

Consciously or unconsciously, you are attracted to and repulsed from individual souls and life events in a similar way a magnet attracts or repels iron filings. Once you stop blaming other people, family circumstances, race, religion, and genetics for the sorrowful situations you may find yourself in during life, you will begin to see that more positive and harmonious attractions will spontaneously manifest in your life.

We are all faced with challenging situations in our lives to overcome. Persons who continue to enter one abusive marriage after another need to accept that they have to change their way of thinking and behavior to alter this negative pattern. An understanding of the Universal Laws can help each of us to learn why we need to create change in our attitudes and personality in order to overcome challenging life situations.

As You Sow, So Shall You Reap

As You Sow, So Shall You Reap is the precursor for the Law of Cause and Effect and the Law of Karma. This law can best be understood if we could view the continuity of the many lifetimes of an individual soul. We would then be able to see the outward effect of a thought or action once set into motion and brought to fruition. But as part of the Divine Plan, we do not retain conscious memories of past lives, so we cannot view the outcome of a specific action begun long ago.

There can be no accidents or mistakes with this law. The corrupt land developer, who destroys natural wild life habitats, or the hunter, who satisfies his lust by killing for sport, will in turn experience the fruits of suffering for these actions. A compassionate act such as feeding the poor, caring for the sick, providing shelter for abused animals, or caring for the natural environment will and must bring about positive results for those souls involved.

As You Sow, So Shall You Reap will definitely produce a reaction equal to the original action. We may not see the result in this lifetime, but it becomes the fabric of your next incarnation.2 Although this reaction will manifest, you can use freedom of choice to make better decisions for future actions. By doing so, you can begin a new phase of attitudes and behaviors with positive and better results. The saying, *"today is the first day of the rest of my life,"* could be adjusted to read *"today is the first day of the rest of my spiritual lives."*

The Law of Cause and Effect

Now we come to the Law of Cause and Effect that can best be associated with our actions and relationships on earth. All interactions on earth have a cause and produce an effect that can be observed manifesting in our daily lives. Cause and Effect is the underlying principle for the other Universal Laws and applies to all of humanity. How it operates can be understood through common everyday situations.

Let's suppose a person has an obesity problem. With the obesity comes feelings of depression, loss of self worth, and isolation because of their appearance and associated health problems. Every diet has been tried with little success. Psychologically, an understanding of why the person overindulges to cause the obesity is usually based on only this life's experiences. But this interpretation may not be adequate to penetrate the root cause for this food addiction.

A deep inner search, including past life events, may provide the key for why food holds this person under its spell. The actual event or lifetime may not be revealed when the food addiction began; but the acceptance that there can be such a reason, emanating from a past life, may allow the person to begin to accept responsibility for overeating in a non-judgmental atmosphere. Instead of blaming current outside circumstances alone, the search for the emotional link to a past lifetime should be explored.

The cause for overeating now might have originated from a lust for food or an opposite reaction to living in extreme poverty in a past lifetime. This individual soul may now be reacting to a past life experience stored in the emotional seed atom, expressing itself through the physical body. To overcome this addiction, quiet spiritual questioning may reveal the root cause of the problem. Then psychological and nutritional programs could be successfully introduced to achieve a more balanced approach to food.

The best approach to living in the world of cause and effect is to acknowledge that what you are today is due to your soul's thoughts, words, and actions from your past lives in association with present life circumstances. Changes towards leading a happier and creative life, in tune with your life's purpose, can result when your inner search includes an understanding of the Universal Laws.

The Law of Karma

Harvey A. Green, in his book, *Life and Death: The Pilgrimage of the Soul,* explains *"Karma is the experiencing of self from one life to the next."*3 Past experiences become part of your soul's evolutionary record carried in your seed atoms, within your soul's bodies, from lifetime to lifetime. The merciful aspect of the Law of Karma is that you do not face all of your challenges in one life. Your individual soul is only expected to encounter certain situations and to repay a manageable portion of your karmic debt during any given life.

Prior to each birth in the after-life, your soul has the opportunity to incorporate into your soul memory the wisdom needed to draw upon what is necessary to experience the consequences that will balance your debts. This is how you are able to face each karmic debt over many lifetimes.

A situation to demonstrate how karmic interactions operate involves a problem that is at epidemic proportions in the United States today. Suppose a drunken driver runs a stop sign, causing a severe car accident with another vehicle. The three occupants in the other car sustain serious and fatal injuries. The driver is immediately killed, his wife becomes paraplegic, and the teenage daughter receives massive head injuries, causing her to permanently lose her sight. The drunken driver, operating a larger vehicle, is barely hurt and sustains only a broken leg.

As the story progresses, the widow is now facing life without her beloved husband and the use of her legs. Bereaved and depressed, she is also the sole provider and caregiver for her blind daughter. The daughter, just three weeks away from graduating from high school with honors, cannot look forward to entering college in the fall. Expensive rehabilitation is her immediate future.

The drunk driver now has an enormous karmic debt to repay, according to the Law of Karma. The driver's careless and selfish attitude is to blame for the suffering caused to this family. If he is sincerely remorseful and prays for God's forgiveness, God will forgive him, but the Law of Karma cannot forgive. For the Law's very nature requires that the debt must be satisfied. To repay his karmic debt, in this life or successive lifetimes, the drunk driver will need to experience accidental death, blindness, loss of a loved one, and paralysis. However, he has some latitude for deciding how many lifetimes he can take to suffer these karmic afflictions.4

This scenario represents the reason why your individual soul continues to reincarnate through many lifetimes within the circle of life and death. It is with this in mind that I give the Law of Karma an entire chapter in which I explain how your karma is not inherited from your ancestors or the result of a whimsical Creator but is a result of your past life actions.

The Law of Grace and Love

Finally, we come to my favorite Law, the Law of Grace and Love. God is infinite knowledge, existence, power, and bliss, and God is also infinite love.5 God, The Universal Oversoul and Infinite Creator of all the worlds and laws, works through the Universal Laws to bring chaos into order.

Scholars throughout history have questioned whether God capriciously doles out Grace, Love, and Mercy by His whim alone. With a limited comprehension of God, it would surely appear that way. But when we open our hearts and minds to the purpose of the Universal Laws, reincarnation, and the ultimate purpose of each individual soul, we can begin to observe the pattern that is God's mercy and love.

A young girl living in an abusive household continues to suffer year after year, while another young girl has a loving family and is encouraged and guided to develop her talents. God, the Universal Mind in His Grace and Love for all creation, hears the prayers of both girls and provides the inner and outer help according to the spiritual needs of each.

We cannot perceive the karma evolving in the lives of each young girl. But through the spiritual perspective, we can begin to understand that God's love is always flowing to all in creation according to their spiritual needs. The development of our spiritual nature is fortified by this love to help us with this spiritual unfoldment. Outer circumstances may need to remain as they are, according to lessons and experiences that we must live through, to fulfill our karmic debts and awaken our consciousness.

Another infinite attribute of God is His unequivocal forgiveness. Forgiveness does not mean that all challenges and obstacles in your life will be mitigated. However, there are times when God, according to His Divine Will and the needs of your soul, will intervene. Plants, animals, and humans are forever within the mindful eye of God. Through your sincere heartfelt prayers, you can at anytime converse with the Oversoul to receive and experience all that you deserve.

The advancing stream of life would not be possible without the Universal Laws functioning to establish order in creation. God, from His Infinite Realm of Reality, brought forth the Universal Laws as a pattern to guide our souls through the spiritual journey to return to Him: *"Godhood is the birthright of every man."*6

Chapter Reflections to Guide Your Spiritual Search

- If you are seeking to create harmonious relationships, first you need to build harmony and peace within your being.

- Universal laws are what guide and keep order in God's creation.

- The Universal Laws are created by God and not by humanity.

- The laws apply equally to all living creatures in creation, not just human beings.

- Laws created by humanity are designed to maintain order in civilization, but they are not perfect and are a poor imitation of God's Universal Laws.

- In a sense, humanity's laws are counterfeit to God's Universal Laws, since they do not represent everyone equally and without prejudice.7

- Unlike God's Universal Laws, laws of the land are changeable, according to the whims of society.

- Society's laws are based in the world of materiality. God's Universal Laws are based in the Reality of God's existence.

References

1. Cayce, Edgar. *Auras,* 5
2. Hall, Manly P. *Death To Rebirth,* 1-15
3. Green, Harvey A. *Life and Death: The Pilgrimage of the Soul,* 49
4. Hall, Manly P. *Reincarnation, The Cycle of Necessity,* 165-168
5. Baba, Meher. *Discourses,* 16-22
6. Baba, Meher. *The Advancing Stream of Life,* 7
7. Green, Harvey A. *Life and Death: The Pilgrimage of the Soul,* 41

   *Green, Harvey A. *Life and Death: The Pilgrimage of the Soul,* 41

6

The Journey of the Soul Through Reincarnation

o o o o o o o o o o o o o o o o o o o o o o o o o o

"It is the sanskit word Samsara that has been translated as reincarnation. Literally the word reincarnation means to incarnate again, to be re-embodied, or more accurately, to be re-enfleshed; to return after death to the physical world in another physical body."

—Manly P. Hall *

Lord Buddha taught that all living things must pass through innumerable re-embodiments until all of the imperfections of the soul's consciousness are removed by experience. Then perfection can be achieved, freeing the soul from the cycle of births and deaths. So why is reincarnation one of the most difficult concepts to accept? Individuals may not believe in reincarnation because their religion does not teach life and death in these terms. Another reason reincarnation is not suitable within the context of one's belief is because it places the responsibility for our experiences of happiness or suffering on our individual selves.

When we study the history of religion before Christianity, we will find the teachings of reincarnation in the ancient religions of Buddhism and Hinduism. Reincarnation was also taught by the Vedantic teachers and Brahmins centuries before the birth of Gautama Buddha. Pythagoras, a Hellenistic philosopher, traveled to India where he became an initiate of Brahmin teachings. In his writings, we find references to his belief in reincarnation and remembrance of his own past lives. Plato, who was influenced by Pythagoras, taught his students that reincarnation was necessary for the soul to perfect the divine nature.1

The church struck reincarnation from the teachings of the Bible, during the sixth century, because it felt it was easier for the congregation to understand Heaven and Hell rather than an existence of multiple lives. Christianity teaches that the actions of an individual's one life, whether good or bad, determines our soul's existence for all of eternity. Why should we have only one chance to get it right in God's kingdom? Even in life, we are given second chances. Ivy O. Duce in her book, *What Am I Doing Here?* describes the doctrine's removal from church teachings.

> *Only the Christian church has failed to teach the truth of reincarnation; all other faiths acknowledge it. And the pity is that the doctrine was taught in the Christian Church until the fifth ecumenical council was held in Constantinople in 543 A.D., at which the Church fathers suddenly decided, and passed a resolution (still on record in the minutes of the meeting), that they would 'no longer teach the doctrine of rebirth.'2*

Dr. Harry L. Kenmore, a New York City chiropractor and spiritual seeker, in a public lecture stated, that the process and functioning of reincarnation exists whether one believes in it or not. If we disbelieve something that does not mean it does not exist. Galileo was criticized for disproving church teachings that the sun, planets, and all of the stars revolved around the earth. Christopher Columbus proved the world to be round by sailing westward to the Americas when society at that time believed the world to be flat. The process and function of gravity existed and influenced creation long before the discovery by Sir Isaac Newton. Darwin's theory of evolution was first ridiculed before it became a prominent theory of our time.

Western man continues to wait for science to give the final word, based on first-hand experiences and observations, on the existence of reincarnation. But the scientific method for studying the spiritual world was utilized by Rudolf Steiner. He developed a scientific approach to attaining knowledge of the higher worlds. He studied the higher worlds as a scientist, calling his approach *"Spiritual Science."* Steiner actually based his findings on his own experience of the supersensible world of spirit. He believed that his ability to know and interact with the hidden world first began through his practice of concentrated meditation. He further believed that others could also attain this level of knowledge and interaction with the spiritual world through three stages of training in the study of spiritual science: imagination, inspiration, and intuition.

> *The first stage gives knowledge of the spiritual background of our physical life and of the world in which we live. The second stage opens the way into the purely supersensible world, giving understanding of its conditions and of the beings who inhabit it, and of their relation to the physical world. The third stage is one in which a man is able to act himself as an inhabitant of the spiritual world, and to have intercourse with those to be found in it.3*

Reincarnation is the process by which karma is worked out. Karma can only be enacted through re-embodiment. This is why reincarnation is a necessary process in the advancing stream of life. Once your individual soul attains the human form, you will not regress back to the animal kingdom.

Normal progression of reincarnation is a forward development of spiritual consciousness for the soul through countless births and deaths. Reincarnation will occur in either the male or female form, depending on the experiences needed and the spiritual requirements to be fulfilled in that lifetime. *"The general advantages and handicaps of an incarnation are always determined by the specific sanskaras the individual soul has accumulated in the past"*4

Without the Law of Reincarnation, we would have to accept that God has created a world where some people live as mentally challenged, paralyzed, blind or abused, while others are rewarded with genius, physical strength, and beauty. Could the talents of Michelangelo, Leonardo DaVinci, Ralph Waldo Emerson, or Albert Einstein develop from only one life experience? And if so, why were their souls the chosen ones for receiving these talents to share with the world?

According to Manly P. Hall, genius is the repetitive improving of talents and abilities over many incarnations of the individual soul. The final culminating incarnation when the talent reaches its peak is due to the soul's ability to recall those previous talents and experiences on a highly refined level. The expression of genius is not dependent on heredity, but uses the genetic make-up inherited from the parents to its advantage for expressing the talents and abilities.

The physical and intellectual aspects of man, his inherent talents and abilities are forged during many hard-earned lives. Genetics reflect the impressions of the inherent characteristics. The parent's genetic make-up and circumstances are chosen by the individual soul for each birth, to provide the incarnating spirit with the circumstances and physical abilities necessary to work out his or her own karma and destiny. The conditions of the incarnation are the responsibility of the individual, carried over from past lives.

> *"In the trance state, Edgar Cayce was apparently able to tap cosmic conscious-ness, and to read the akashic records on which are supposedly written the total history of each soul from the beginning of time. Akasha is a Sanskrit word for which there is no English equivalent. It refers to the impressionable records of all thought forms and experiences in the history of mankind."*[5]

As a result of his life readings, many people became convinced of the existence of reincarnation. They were also able to understand and seek relief from physical and mental afflictions originating from past lives. Cayce's descriptions of past life actions and their link to present circumstances rang true for them.

Meher Baba describes how the individual soul assumes various physical forms in order for the soul's consciousness to expand and to experience everything there is to experience. We are unable to progress from one level of consciousness to another without experiencing the previous level. This can only be accomplished through the process of reincarnation, as the soul and its consciousness awakens through the experiences of the different forms.

The unconscious soul, through experiences of all types, finally arrives at full consciousness to answer the question, Who am I? I am God. This is the destiny of every soul in creation.

Reincarnation in the cycle of life and death will then cease for each individual soul when this evolutionary goal of perfection and expansion of consciousness is complete. To achieve the goal of perfection, each life's purpose, while on earth, needs to be fulfilled. This is the karma for each life. This process of rebirth will repeat over and over until one arrives at full consciousness and all of life's lessons are learned.

By applying spiritual scientific methods and awakening our spiritual intuition, we can raise our consciousness to higher levels and explore the realms of the saints, mystics, and masters. Through opening our spiritual faculties to the higher levels of the intuitive world within, answers to the haunting questions of life and rebirth can become accessible to us, as spirit beings. The spiritual world, which lies beyond our five senses, is waiting to be discovered.

> *There is, perhaps, no philosophical doctrine in the world that has so mag-nificent an intellectual ancestry as that of Reincarnation—the unfolding of the human Spirit through recurrent lives on earth, experience being gathered during the earth life and worked up into intellectual faculty and conscience*

during the heaven–life, so that a child is born with his past experiences trans-muted into mental and moral tendencies and powers.6

Chapter Reflections to Guide Your Spiritual Search

- Reincarnation is the chain that links each individual soul's karma through all lifetimes.

- Belief in reincarnation dispels fear of death and eases the grief of bereavement, since those loved ones who precede us in death will be encountered many times again.7

- Your spirit, through countless lifetimes, will gain higher levels of consciousness until your individual soul with full consciousness is reunited with God.

- When parents learn to identify their children's latent talents, they are in a position to support and guide their spiritual and intellectual growth.

- Genius is the repetitive improving of talents and abilities over many incarnations of the individual soul.

- *"New knowledge, easily gained, is old knowledge"*. Plato

- *"Did I not live in another body, or somewhere else, before entering my mother's womb?"* Confessions of St. Augustine, 1:6.

References

1. Montgomery, Ruth. *Here and Hereafter*, 79-81
2. Duce, Ivy O. *What Am I Doing Here?*, 24
3. Shepherd, A.P. *A Scientist of the Invisible*, 63
4. Baba, Meher. *Discourses*, 320
5. Montgomery, Ruth. *Here and Hereafter*, 86
6. Besant, Annie. *The Riddle of Life*, 28
7. Montgomery, Ruth. *Here and Hereafter*, 78

   *Hall, Manly P. *Reincarnation: The Cycle of Necessity*, 15

7

Remembering Our Past Lives

○ ○

"Mohanda K. Gandhi wrote to Madeleine Slade, daughter of a distinguished British admiral, who became one of Gandhi's disciples: " What you say about rebirth is sound. It is nature's kindness that we do not remember past births. What is the good either of knowing in detail the numberless births we have gone through? Life would be a burden if we carried such a tremendous load of memories. A wise man deliberately forgets many things, even as a lawyer forgets the cases and their details as soon as they are disposed of. Yes, 'death is but a sleep and a forgetting.' If death is not a prelude to another life, the intermediate period is a cruel mockery."

—Mohanda Gandhi *

Many people ask if reincarnation exists, then why can't I remember my past lives? There is a saying; *"with the good comes the bad."* Our natural tendency only wants to remember the good and pleasant aspects of previous incarnations. We want to think of ourselves as great personalities, living in happiness with the people we loved and the accomplishments we attained. We would not want to remember ourselves as ordinary, or worse, as unsavory characters, miserably living in poverty and abusive relationships. In addition, remembering our past lives would complicate living in the present life. This is why the Law of Grace inhibits the memories of past incarnations from infiltrating our present memories.

Imagine in your past life that you died on the U.S.S. Arizona. It was Sunday, 8:00 AM, December 7, 1941, Pearl Harbor, Hawaii. You were asleep below deck. Suddenly, a huge explosion rocks the ship and awakens you; water begins to rush into the compartment. There you remain for two weeks, trapped in an air pocket with your bunkmates slowly dying of thirst, starvation, and oxygen deprivation. You vainly bang out on the bulkhead in Morse code, "We are alive; get us out!" One thousand and seventy seven men lost their lives on the Arizona that day, many of them immediately. The cause was one Japanese bomb that penetrated the forward deck exploding the ammunitions bunker.

This scenario represents a horrific experience in the life of an individual soul. If this memory was carried over into the mental body as a clear and detailed memory of the event, imagine how difficult it would be for the soul to psychologically move forward in his or her current life. One would be fixated on the feelings, bunkmates, and the enemy who was responsible for the tragedy. Instead, we carry over vague, abstract feelings associated with events of past lives, stored in our subtle and mental seed atoms.

Individuals in their present incarnation have a hard enough time dealing with emotions and events that happen in their current life. Growing up in an abusive family situation, experiences of war as a youth, or a survivor of the World Trade Center disaster leaves a scarred memory tying one to the past. Just imagine if this was compounded by similar past life memories mixing together turbulent emotions and thoughts. One would never be able to move beyond the emotional trauma. However, the thoughts and emotions of past lives are stored in our memory as impressions that unconsciously influence the development of our present personality.

Edgar Cayce has noted many times in his discourses about past life memories, that each individual becomes the sum total of all of his or her previous experiences with fragments of past life memories frequently coming to the surface in every day life.

Manly P. Hall continues to describe how past life-memories can reach our conscious mind in a present life.

> *What is called life is just a small, visible part of the ages, the epilogue of the drama of yesterday. Most people will find that their past life comes to them in their present incarnation chiefly as unfinished business. Also, as each person*

goes down the years, flashes of the past come to him. He meets someone whom
he has known before. He stands in some place where he knows he has stood
before. He reads a book about some past civilization and feels that he has
lived and labored in that very age the book describes.1

Unconscious memories might be triggered in the present life by feelings arising from certain odors, a specific house, a painting, or a poem. The activities, places, and people we may be drawn to can also be past life connections. Unexplained animosity to a coworker or a strong attraction to a new acquaintance is another indication that there is a link beyond current circumstances.2

Everyone remembers a friend or relative telling the story of a person who is having such bad dreams that they cannot sleep, or the person who is so afraid to go on an airplane that this behavior is interfering with their career. Such dreams and fears can sometimes be the memories of recent past lives leaking into the conscious part of our mind in this present incarnation.

People we have never met or places we have never been in this incarnation may be a part of a dream sequence. When we wake up from the dream, we are curious about the people and places we have seen. Past life memories find their way into our dreams through our subconscious. Meher Baba has stated that people, places, and incidents that reoccur in our sleep-dream state, which we have no recollection of when we are awakened, are people and places from a past life which have seeped through that thin veil separating the subconscious and conscious mind. This veil is especially vulnerable when we are children.

Dreams might also bring with them unpleasant memories. Growing up in the 1950's, I had a friend who had reoccurring nightmares of a terrifying event. He would dream of falling through the atmosphere with flames all around him. This was brought to Meher Baba's attention when he was visiting Myrtle Beach, South Carolina, in 1956. He clearly stated to my friend's parents that in his last incarnation, he was a pilot in World War II who was shot down and killed. Once the underlying cause of the nightmares was revealed to my friend, they no longer disturbed him.

When someone asked Edgar Cayce, during his trance state, about remembering past lives, he stated, *"we don't have to remember, we are the sum total of all our memories."* Many young souls come into the world with fears that cannot be explained: fear of fire, explosions, small spaces, flying, water, and the list goes on. Doctors try to find out the causes for these fears only in this life, instead of exploring the possibility that the fear might have originated through the type of death the soul experienced in their past life.3

Habits or idiosyncrasies, likes and dislikes, talents, physical and emotional strengths or weaknesses can all be part of past-life characteristics. Some people even believe that birth marks or a slight limp might be remnants of wounds or injuries from another incarnation, seeping through into the present. Many of these past life characteristics and physical attributes penetrate the veil at an early age in our lives. Edgar Cayce terms this the continuity of life.

Manly P. Hall has stated,

> *The best way for the average person to measure what he has been in the past life is to examine the qualities he brings with him into this life. Each person has special abilities, interests and indifferences, likes and dislikes tastes and aversions. All these characteristics are the records of what has been experienced in the past.*4

The book, *The Reincarnation of Famous People*, by Kevin J. Todeschi, based on the Edgar Cayce readings, states that one can be famous in one life; but in the next, they are just another ordinary person. A great deal of this continuity of life depends on the parents that we choose for this lifetime. Are they open minded enough to be aware that talents that are resurfacing from a previous life need to be encouraged and nurtured for the sake of the soul's continued development? Without this nurturing the latent talents and abilities from a soul's bank of intuitive wisdom may not manifest and may even inhibit the development of the present life's purpose.

Remembering one's past lives naturally can be an avenue to overcome the obstacles manifesting in your present life. It is best not to uncover all aspects of your past lives artificially; however, if memories do seep through, try to use them in solving problems and relating them to your present life difficulties. Through quiet reflection, intuitive answers will come forward from the spirit or spark of God within.

As we advance on the spiritual path, we should be developing the tendency to keep track of our spiritual accomplishments gained over many lifetimes, rather than the accomplishments of worldly fame and material gain. For it is the former which will release us from our suffering and the circle of life and death. We never lose the distilled wisdom of all our life experiences. It is the totality of our spiritual accomplishments and wisdom that will eventually awaken our spiritual intuition and consciousness to higher levels.5

Chapter Reflections to Guide Your Spiritual Search

- When experiencing extreme emotional distress, try to find the cause by recalling past life memories through quiet reflection and sincere prayer.

- You may recall memories when you see a place, inhale a certain fragrance, or have a feeling, which will stir your mind into a replay of a detailed memory. Just let it happen, let your imagination run and see where it leads.

- In each lifetime, we are born with a new physical brain, which on its own has no memories of the past.6 The seed atoms store the impressions that can be released as memories into our bloodstream.7

- *"Under ordinary circumstances, only the memories of the present life can appear in consciousness because the new brain acts as a hindrance to the release of the memories of those experiences which had to be gathered through the medium of other brains in past lives."*8

- Fears you are experiencing may be left over from a past life. Part of your life's purpose may deal with overcoming the fears. People who fear water, fire, or confined spaces could have died in a drowning incident, a plane crash, or a mine cave-in in another lifetime.

- We carry over many characteristics, habits, and emotions, both positive and negative, from our past lives. We should learn to improve upon the positive and annihilate the negative.

- Reoccurring dreams can be a seepage of a past life experience. Taylor Caldwell wrote the book, *The Romance of Atlantis*, based on past life memories and dreams of her lifetime in the fabled continent of Atlantis.

References

1. Hall, Manly P. *Questions and Answers*, 97-98
2. Todeschi, Kevin J. *Edgar Cayce on the Akashic Records*, 11
3. Langley, Noel. *Edgar Cayce on Reincarnation*, 109-111
4. Hall, Manly P. *Questions and Answers*, 97
5. Todeschi, Kevin. *Akashic Records*, 131-132
6. Hall, Manly P. *Reincarnation: The Cycle of Necessity*, 167
7. Chaney, Earlyne. *The Mystery of Death and Dying*, 26-28
8. Baba, Meher. *The Advancing Stream of Life*, 73

    *Montgomery, Ruth. *Here and Hereafter*, 81

8

Karma and the Soul's Destiny

"Again the specter raised a cry, and shook his chain and wrung his shadowy hands. "You are fettered," said Scrooge trembling. "Tell me why?" "I wear the chain I forged in life," replied the Ghost. "Made it link by link, and yard by yard; I girded it on of my own free will, and of my own free will I wore it…"

—Charles Dickens *

Edgar Cayce stated that karma is *"patterns of memory;"* it is the concept that people are constantly meeting themselves, through relationships and actions with other individual souls from their past.1 Karma is a Sanskrit word which means, work, deed or action; it can also be translated as cause and effect. The Law of Cause and Effect is a Universal Law in the physical world, and karma is the Universal Law of the spiritual realm. This is the basic concept of karma in our life of values and morals. Karma is the unifying law of the Universe that enables us, through reincarnation, to reach our final purpose in life, which is union with God.

Manly P. Hall, in his book, *Reincarnation: The Cycle of Necessity*, uses a quote from Madame H.P. Blavatsky to explain how the concept of karma can be the only way to understand good and evil in the world of values and morals.

> *"It is only the knowledge of the constant rebirths of one and the same individuality throughout the life cycle…that can explain to us the mysterious problem of Good and Evil, and reconcile man to the terrible and apparent injustice of life. Nothing but such certainty can quiet our revolted sense of justice. For, when one unacquainted with the noble doctrine looks around him, and observes the inequalities of birth and fortune, of intellect and capacities; when one sees honor paid fools and profligates, on whom fortune has heaped her favors by mere priviledge of birth, while their nearest neighbor with all his intellect and noble virtues—far more deserving in every way—perishing of want and for lack of sympathy; when one sees all this and has to turn away, helpless to relieve the undeserved suffering, one's ears ringing and heart aching with the cries of pain around him—that blessed knowledge of Karma alone prevents him from cursing life and men, as well as their supposed creator."2*

Even with the understanding of karma and the *"patterns of memory,"* we still may have a difficult time believing that the universe is just, especially when justice cannot be observed soon after an evil action is done. But as we all observe, an acorn will definitely grow into the oak tree in time. According to the Law of Karma, evil will rebound on the evil doer, even if it takes a series of lifetimes.

A friend once told me a story of how she and her husband were swindled out of money in a scam. They tried all legal avenues to get the money returned but to no avail. One day, the wife commented, "It never seems that people like that ever get punished. They go through life without the consciousness of how their actions hurt other individuals." My friend was Catholic and did not believe in reincarnation. I asked her to take a look around at the people who are born with terrible physical, emotional, and mental afflictions. Did God just choose to punish these people for fun? The Law of Karma clearly shows that God does not punish people. People punish themselves by their own actions through *"patterns of memory"* from previous lifetimes. They may do something in one life and then have to pay for it in the next. No one should fear God, but fear their own actions when they cause suffering to others.

I went on to explain to my friend, "You should do all you can to bring a person to justice, in accordance with the laws of society, then just leave the results to God. The Law of Karma will right the wrong, if not in this life then in another lifetime." Those of us who accept reincarnation and the Law of Karma accept this means of repayment for what one has done in a previous life. So, I said to my friend, "Your scam artists will have to experience the suffering of losing money in a similar way that caused you to suffer because of your loss. From a spiritual perspective, God does forgive all sins and mistakes of an individual soul, if you are remorseful; but The Law of Karma does not forgive and demands reimbursement."

In understanding the Law of Karma, we need to accept that even young children suffering from physical and emotional abuse, accidents, or disease in some cases may be looked upon as receiving karmic retribution for things they did in their previous lives. At this age, they are still too young to use free will or make choices in the present life. Their emotional body is still insufficiently developed to incur new negative impressions. So the karma causing their suffering would need to be coming from their actions in a previous life.

> *The karmic law does not come to the spirit as the oppressiveness of some external or blind power, but is something involved in the rationality of the scheme of life. Karmic determination is the condition of true responsibility. It means that a man will reap as he sows.3*

As I explained to my friends, "A person who has committed an evil action will have to accept the consequence and a person who does a good deed must be rewarded, whether they believe in the Law of Karma or not." Meher Baba said, "*What he does for another, he also has done for himself, although it may take time for him to realize that this is exactly so. The Law of Karma is an expression of justice and a reflection of the unity of life in the world of duality.*"4

So who is responsible for our suffering and the injustice in the world of duality? In *The Holy Bible* there is a passage that answers the question, when understood in its original concept. "*The Lord is long-suffering and of great mercy, forgiving iniquity and transgression, and by no means clearing the guilty, visiting the iniquity of the fathers upon the children unto the third and fourth generation.*"5 Accepting the concept of *The Holy Bible* in this format would have you believe that God is unjust and unloving to all in creation. Are we to inherit and live one life in the shadow of our ancestor's mistakes?

Earlyne Chaney, in her book, *The Mystery of Death and Dying* explains this alteration of the concept of our ancestor's iniquities.

> *To harmonize with the wisdom teachings, the scripture should read that the karma of the "father" is visited upon the "child" unto the fourth incarnation, not generation. The mistakes you made in the last four incarnations may be visited upon you in the form of karma flowing out of the heart seed atom in the present generation. Thus what you "fathered," or created, in your last incarnation may be the source ("parent") of your karma today. You are a child of that parent today. You have inherited from that parent—the you of the past, not your physical parents—all of your characteristics, weaknesses and strengths.6*

Our past is reflected in our karma in the present. Relationships from our past are repeated in varying degrees in the future. Chances are relationships from past lifetimes are not necessarily the same. A parent-child role might be reversed. The relationships we have with individuals for any given life are a reflection of the karma of our soul connections from the past. Once again, as Edgar Cayce has stated, *"Karma is simply patterns of memory."* The patterns manifest because memory is stored in our immortal consciousness. Memories associated with thoughts and faculties of thinking are stored in our mental seed atom in the mental body. Emotions, desires, and character strengths and weaknesses are brought with us in our emotional (astral) seed atom in the subtle body. The total record of all our memories—which include all thoughts, emotions and actions from all our past lives—are kept in our heart seed atom, located in the area of our physical heart.

> *The heart seed atom, containing its perpetual record of your past, ties you to your karmic destiny, while the mental and astral seed atoms, containing the characteristic powers or weaknesses, enable you to control your future, your own destiny. Thus you have two seed atoms subject to your free will and a destiny of your own choosing—and you have one seed atom securely holding you to your karmic past destiny and "fate."*7

Although we bring *"patterns of memory"* with us to each life, the karmic continuity of life may be modified through the process of freedom of choice through the mental and emotional (astral) seed atoms. Even before karma is created between individual souls, there is the freedom of choice to determine the type of relationship that will emerge. But once that relationship is begun, karma is started. *"The rhythm in which two souls start their relationship tends to perpetuate itself unless the souls, through fresh intelligent karma, change the rhythm and raise it to a higher quality."*8

Suppose two individual souls meet, fall in love, and marry. But what happens if the relationship becomes dysfunctional, due to individual karmic issues of jealousy and selfishness. This can lead to a destructive ending to the once star-struck lovers. Fortunately for the couple, one of them may turn inwardly to call out silently for guidance. This silent call guides them, through inner prompting, to get their relationship back on a positive track with counseling, prayer, and mutual respect. They met due to the Law of Attraction and Karma; now through freedom of choice and the Law of Grace, they are able to alter their dysfunctional behavior pattern to create a more harmonious relationship.

If the couple continued on their destructive path, further mental and physical abuse might be the outcome. At that point in time, they would not be ready to resolve their karmic differences peacefully. Divorce would be the best strategy to prevent more destructive karmic patterns between them. It would be best for them to separate in this lifetime and meet again in a later incarnation as more mature souls. If this pattern coming through the heart seed atom were to continue in this current chaotic loop, one partner might be compelled to murder the other in a rage of passion and anger. Therefore, they would be creating more binding karmic ties for the future. Through the emotional and mental seed atoms, they would have the capacity to accept the Law of Grace and offset the negative karma.

We should try to remember that when our individual soul enters human consciousness, it has to gain experiences on earth as part of the process of reincarnation. In the beginning of the soul's journey it does not matter what experiences the soul goes through or in what order. As the soul increases consciously, making spiritual gains, a more intelligent selection is needed to refine the experiences. This could be compared to a child going from kindergarten to graduation in high school. There are the basic experiences, relationships, and actions the individual soul must learn. It is only when the individual enters college that one can begin to choose the course of study to prepare for a career.

Esoterically, earth existence has been called the school of life. Only in the physical world do we gain experience through interaction with other individual souls. This cannot be done in the after-life where existence is subjective. One could refer to the after-life or in-between life state of existence, as summer vacation for the soul to reflect on lessons learned. As we make more intelligent choices on earth, our consciousness is elevated to higher spiritual levels, propelling us toward our goal with less interference from negative experiences. Our karma is then said to be evolving in a more spiritual direction.

At some point we ask ourselves, how can I begin to turn towards a spiritual direction and at the same time create more happiness in my life? When this happens, we start to approach life and death with a new perspective. We gradually incorporate new spiritual principles into our daily lives. Our intuitive side begins to awaken to the spiritual path ahead. Mystic and spiritual seekers refer to the soul turning inward, towards the path home, as involution.

> *"Every man is in the place he has earned for himself; every man is doing the same thing he has earned the right to do; no one is suffering for the mistakes of others, but for his own mistakes. The only way to be happy, therefore, is to live well, thus setting in action constructive cycles of cause and effect. If we want to be wise, we must earn wisdom. Every individual who lives in the world is in the place he has earned for himself by his actions in this or previous lives."*9

Chapter Reflections to Guide Your Spiritual Search

- Your karma in this life is the result of your deeds from your past four lifetimes.[10]

- Every sixth lifetime, the soul is given a 'respite' from its karmic journey. You will be born into a life of extreme ease. How you use your time, money, and creative energies towards helping others in that life will determine any positive or negative spiritual progress.[11]

- When we harm or kill another human being through malice or anger, we will have to experience those same actions in a future lifetime. This is karmic justice.

- Every soul has the capacity through the emotional and mental seed atoms to change their impressions through the use of their free will and God's Grace.

- Awakening your spiritual intuition, through the use of prayer, helps you to meet your karmic debt with a brave heart. Such debts might manifest during your life as an illness, physical, emotional or mental disability, crisis in a relationship, or a loss of financial security.

- It is spiritually appropriate to assist individual souls who are suffering, regardless of how the suffering was incurred.

- Consciously strive to develop your positive strengths and creative tendencies for a better karmic future.

References

1. Todeschi, Kevin J. *Edgar Cayce on the Akashic Records*, 11
2. Hall, Manly P. *Reincarnation: The Cycle of Necessity*, 9
3. Hall, Manly P. *Questions and Answers*, 97
4. Baba, Meher. *Discourses*, 333
5. *The Holy Bible*, Numbers 14:18
6. Chaney, Earlyne. *The Mystery of Death and Dying*, 24
7. Chaney, Earlyne. *The Mystery of Death and Dying*, 21
8. Baba, Meher. *Discourses*, 330
9. Hall, Manly P. *Questions and Answers*, 86
10. Chaney, Earlyne. *The Mystery of Death and Dying*, 24
11. Langley, Noel. *Edgar Cayce on Reincarnation*, 93

  *Dickens, Charles. *Christmas Books Centennial Edition. A Christmas Carol*, 24

PART 3
The Development of Consciousness

9

Sanskaras, the DNA of Karma

o o o o o o o o o o o o o o o o o o o o o o o o

"Every experience the soul-consciousness has makes an impression. These impressions are called "sanskaras" by many people in India and Far Eastern countries. Impressions (sanskaras) come from everything one experiences – you can look at a sunset and be exalted by its beauty. That leaves an impression. A person can hit you physically and it leaves an impression. A person can say something nice or nasty and that leaves an impression. You can even get an impression in dreams."

—*Ivy O. Duce* *

Sanskaras is a Sanskrit word, which translates into *"impressions."* Sanskaras are created through earthly experiences and stored in the seed atoms of the subtle and mental bodies of the soul. Past life sanskaras return with us to each new earth incarnation to be expended. In the process of expending them, we create new sanskaras. Our impressions cannot be worn out in the astral realm of the after death-state, so we are drawn back to earth by our karmic impressions.

How can new sanskaras be created? They can be created in two ways: subjective mental processes, which involve already existing impressions in the ego-mind, and objective impressions gathered through new physical experiences. The ego-mind creates subjective sanskaras during the thinking process using existing thoughts to understand and evaluate that which it has already experienced. Objective sanskaras are gathered when a thought, desire, or action is put into motion by the ego.1

I use an analogy: sanskaras are the DNA of karma to describe the nature of sanskaras. As DNA expresses the genetic code, sanskaras manifest the karmic code. In other words, sanskaras determine every karmic aspect of our character and personality—our physical, emotional, and mental profile in each lifetime. We choose our parents for their hereditary characteristics that match the sanskaras needed for expression in our life. Every aspect of our physical appearance, race, nationality, religion, health, and the socio-economic status we are born into are determined in this way.

If you are born with a specific affliction because of a karmic debt, it is the sanskaras which determine the type of affliction—physical, emotional or mental, the time it will manifest in your lifetime, how long it will last, and the level of its severity. This is all built into the initial matrix of your incarnating soul as you re-enter your mother's womb. It is the function of your ego-mind to organize your sanskaras so that conflicting impressions in your consciousness will not create chaos when they compete for expression.2

When you reincarnate, you come down to earth with a specific set of sanskaras for that lifetime, chosen with your Guardian Angel prior to your rebirth. This is just a small grouping from your overall pool of karmic impressions, usually carried over from any of your past four incarnations. Only when you are living in the physical world can this karma be worked out. But you cannot work out all your karma in one lifetime.

All past impressions recorded in the subconscious heart seed atom will not find expression all at once. We are born with all of our positive and negative sanskaras. Lucky for us, the bulk of these impressions usually can stay dormant until the right lifetime is chosen for their expression. However, the impressions that represent the animalistic, instinctive side of our nature can leak out, especially when we use our free will to express the lower level of our character. This is the Mr. Hyde of the Dr. Jeckle. We can see the expression of this side of humanity most readily when emotions are allowed to dominate over reason.

Civilization on earth today is inhabited by individual souls on various spiritual levels. This mixture of people represents a wide spectrum of souls from the animalistic/material consciousness to the spiritual/elevated consciousness. Some people create good for humanity, animals, and nature through self-sacrifice; while other people indulge in lust, greed, cruelty, and anger at extreme levels. All are living together on earth during this Kali Yuga period in history.3

This is a very difficult time in earth's history because of this extreme mix of humanity on different spiritual levels. Normally, according to esoteric teachings, before recorded history, only one level of humanity existed during each specific period or epoch. Spiritually minded people with high moral values and barbaric people without moral values and order in their culture never existed together.4

An example of low sanskaric consciousness can be found in the gang and terrorist mentality that exists in the world today. Seeking territory, inflicting pain, causing violence and death to all that oppose them satisfies their lustful, animalistic sanskaras. They do harm without a consciousness of moral right or wrong. Dr. Harry L. Kenmore, referred to this type of person, at this stage of consciousness, as a hum-animal. They are physically human beings whose ego-mind is functioning through their animalistic sanskaras. They are souls of young evolution who have no place in the civilized world to act out their animalistic impressions. They have a difficult time coexisting in a highly civilized society where a code of ethics and morals is expected. Gradually, they will incarnate repeated times and process the experiences in their after-life to gain enough good sanskaras to cause their karma and actions to change.5

This concept of humanity differs somewhat from Christian thought. Christians believe that souls who have lived an evil life will end up in hell for all eternity. By understanding spiritual teachings and the advancing stream of life, we see that all souls on earth progress through the evolution of consciousness and must have a chance to gain good sanskaras to raise their consciousness to a higher level. The Laws of Reincarnation and God's Grace function to make this possible.

The consciousness of those who have lived an evil life begins to change because in the after-life they will experience a form of hell state as a result of the Universal Laws of Cause and Effect and What You Sow, So Shall You Reap. The natural order of Creation allows these souls in the after-life to experience the suffering they have inflicted from the viewpoint of their victims.6 They will also have to reincarnate, as a consequence of this karmic debt, into many lifetimes of misery, and experience the torture and abuse they caused to other individual souls. Only in this way, through this type of suffering, can their consciousness develop a moral code and begin to seek good experiences. I have come to realize that viewing individual suffering from a limited perspective of the one life inhibits our spiritual understanding of how life and death are intertwined.

This awakening of consciousness is what is termed *"developing a conscience or superego"* by modern psychology. In future incarnations when young souls are tempted to execute an evil act, the reminder of the karmic debt of suffering, now housed as an impression in their subconscious mind (of the soul's mental body), becomes their conscience. The soul will unconsciously draw on these memories of suffering that it experienced and curtail evil actions now and in the future. In this way, the individual soul slowly turns away from acting out of its impulsive and emotional sanskaras and through intellect and right decisions begins to build a new set of sanskaras to draw from in life.

Whether a soul is young or old the process of gaining positive impressions in childhood is the responsibility of the parents. According to Inayat Khan and Rudolph Steiner, parents need to guide their children towards ethical and moral behavior to foster spiritual growth. The home environment should encourage the development of positive impressions. Parents also have the opportunity to bring out the best in themselves for their karmic future when they nurture their children in a spiritual environment.

The first seven years of a child's life is so important. It is during this time that the child is most impressionable for spiritual growth. This means that one of the parents needs to spend time with the growing infant to ensure that a loving and spiritual life is fostered. If at all possible, a child should not be exposed to a lot of adult strangers, such as in a day care environment, where children may be treated as a commodity by paid employees whose spiritual inclinations may not coincide with the parents.

Also, children for the first seven years are linked to the angelic realm and need to be gradually introduced to the world. Inayat Khan says in his teachings that the subtle/emotional body of the child's individual soul is still not developed in the first seven years of its lifetime. This is a time for the parents to guide the infant to develop its *"life's rhythm"* through quietude, love, routine and the exposure to the finer qualities of a spiritual life.

He further explains that during the first seven years, the child's impressions lay dormant. The infant's individual soul is like an *"unexposed photographic negative."* The first seven years of exposure to external impressions will determine how children will function when their own impressions begin to activate. Prior to the seventh year, the child does not experience right or wrong. Therefore, the parents must be extremely careful to guide and nurture the child through these years. The parent's value system can only be imparted if they are interacting with the child. Inayat Khan explains how to develop the character of a child.

> It is a great mistake when everyone in the family tries to train or to take care of the infant, because that keeps an infant from forming a character. Each one has his own influence, and each influence is different from the other.

But, most often, what happens is that the parents never think of education in infancy. They think that is the age when the child is a doll, a toy; that everyone can handle it and play with it. They do not think that is the most important moment in the soul's life; that never again that opportunity will come for a soul to develop.7

Once the child reaches seven years old, the individual begins to function through the emotional /subtle body. The child's own sanskaras begin to function to manifest behavior. Parents are sometimes surprised at this junction. Their child's personality changes greatly. This happens again at the age of fourteen or at puberty, when the mental body comes into play. Interestingly, many societies unconsciously determine adulthood at twenty-one years of age when the mental body is fully developed. It is at this age that all three soul bodies are now functioning and interacting as one with the physical form. The individual soul capable of using free will becomes solely responsible for all actions, both to society and karmically (as determined by past sanskaras).

Sanskaras, the DNA of karma, are at the spiritual core of who we are as human beings. They are the spiritual codes residing in the subtle and mental bodies that create our physical genetic matrix for each lifetime. Genetics, the biological code, interprets the sanskaric information to determine our physical, emotional, and mental composition in life. We are constantly creating and recreating ourselves with each new impression. In this way, through God's Grace and free will, we are in a unique position each day to strive towards perfection.

"All impressions of joy, sorrow, fear, disappointment become engraved on the mind. This means that they have become man's self. In other words, man is the record of his impressions. The religion of old said that the record of man's actions will be reproduced on the last day, that angels write down all the good and ill done by each person. What we learn from this allegorical expression is that all is impressed on the mind. Although it is forgotten, it is always there, and it will one day show itself."8

Chapter Reflections to Guide Your Spiritual Search

- Every aspect of our physical appearance, race, nationality, religion, health, and the socio-economic status we are born into are determined by sanskaras prior to our birth.

- Infants remain in the aura of the parents for the first seven years.

- We are constantly creating and recreating ourselves with each new impression.

- Exposure to violent movies and video games imparts negative impressions that will need to be expended at some point. If you want happiness and beauty in your life, expose yourself to harmonious and beautiful influences.

- When one shows love and kindness to animals and other creatures of the lower kingdoms, one, in turn, is gaining positive impressions for their future lives.

References

1. Baba, Meher. *Discourses,* 32-39
2. Baba, Meher. *Discourses,* 328-329
3. Cerminara, Gina. *Many Mansions,* 68-69
4. Alder, Vera Stanley. *The Fifth Dimension and the Future of Mankind,* 28-36
5. Kenmore, Harry L. *Lecture Series,* no. 5
6. Baba, Meher. *Discourses,* 309-312
7. Khan, Inayat. *Education,* 3
8. Khan, Inayat. *Spiritual Dimension of Psychology,* 189

*Duce, Ivy O. *What Am I Doing Here,* 7

10

The Influence of Thoughts on Our Consciousness

♦

Thoughts Are Things

o o o o o o o o o o o o o o o o o o o o o o o o

"I hold it true that thoughts are things;
They're endowed with bodies and breath and wings;
And we send them forth to fill
The world with good results, or ill.
That which we call our secret thought
Speeds forth to earth's remotest spot,
Leaving its blessings or its woes
Like tracks behind it as it goes.

We build our future, thought by thought,
For good or ill, yet know it not.
Yet, so the universe was wrought.
Thought is another name for fate;
Choose, then, thy destiny and wait,
For love brings love and hate brings hate."

—Author unknown. *

We all believe in electricity each time we turn on our lights. Although we cannot see the flow of the electrons traveling through space in the wires, we see the result when the light bulb turns the room bright. The Rosicrucian's have a phrase, *"thoughts are things,"* implying a similar movement of thoughts through space just as a stream of electrons creates electricity.

Too many people view the idea of thoughts traveling through space and penetrating our bodies as a *"psychic phenomenon"*. They seem afraid to accept thought transference as a natural occurrence and part of the invisible world that we cannot perceive with our physical senses.1 Everyone has experienced suddenly thinking of someone, a friend or relative, with whom we have not communicated for a long time. Soon after our thoughts, we get an email or phone call from the very person we had been thinking about. "Hi Larry, it's John, you know I have been thinking about you all day…" The thought of your friend was not generated by your own mind. You received his thoughts of you as they traveled to your mental body.

How do we differentiate from the floating thoughts and feelings from other people and our own thoughts and intuition? Outside floating thoughts, our own thoughts and intuition all come to us as inner voices that evoke happiness or sorrow. This inner voice may not be our intuition that we hear but thoughts passing through our mind from outside influences or thoughts from our mind. Intuition comes from the depths of our own inner self and remains with us; it is not fleeting.

> *"It is not easy to recognize an intuition. The thought waves are just like voice waves. It is quite possible for the thought of another person to float into that field of which one is conscious, and hearing it one may think it is one's intuition."2*

Intuition is universal knowledge that is beyond the limited worldly knowledge and therefore beyond the scope of human consciousness or mind. In other words, the thoughts from our mind can only produce knowledge from the world of the five senses. Intuition is a sixth sense and therefore can only be awakened from the depth of our spirit being. It develops as a spiritual knowledge of how things will turn out in the future, a surety of results. It comes to us as this feeling or the *"little voice in our head."* Meher Baba describes how to recognize an intuition.

> *When you feel something as intuition and have no doubt about it, then know it is real. Passing doubtful thoughts and temporary emotional feelings should not be given importance. But when you feel it touches your heart, follow it. When it is from the mind, it is not intuition. Intuition means that which*

comes from the heart. In the divine path, first there is intuition, then inspiration, then illumination, and finally Realization. If it touches your heart, follow it.3

A person who believes in and uses the power of spiritual intuition, positive thinking, and affirmations elevates their consciousness to guide their life to unfold in the way they imagine it. Every person acts as a thought generator. We are all capable of positive or negative thoughts, depending on our upbringing and the sanskaric pool of impressions that we bring with us to earth in each lifetime. How much energy we give to positive or negative thoughts depends on our level of spiritual development and free will. When you think of a sick friend, you imagine your friend getting well. These thoughts will create a positive influence when your friend receives them. The Rosicrucians' teach, *"every time we think a thought, we are making a thought form which may become a living force."* Your thought forms of love will aid recovery of your friend.

Negative thought forms could also influence our lives and those around us. Anger, hate, lust, fear, and greed all give rise to negative thought forms. These living forms of thought can harm us by undermining the constructive forces in our life. We can also hurt others by dwelling on revengeful thoughts. In the long run, we are creating a negative karmic binding for our own future. Remember the child's rhyme *"sticks and stones may break my bones but words can never harm me."* Thought forms can harm you if you are not aware of their influence from this spiritual perspective. *"As you think, so shall you be. So flush out all old, tired, worn-out thoughts. Fill your mind with fresh, new, creative thoughts of faith, love, and goodness. By this process you can actually remake your life"* as expressed by Norman Vincent Peale.4

It is sometimes difficult to keep positive intuitive thoughts in our lives when we are constantly in close proximity with other people. In city environments, there is an intermingling of thought auras, especially in apartment living. Your thought auras are intermingling with the thought auras of your neighbors. Their thought influence becomes stronger because of their close proximity. Depending on who your neighbors are, you can feel tired, depressed, and confused, due to the hundreds of different thought forms bombarding your mind and physical body. By understanding the nature of thought transference, one can differentiate between your own positive, intuitive thoughts and those of outside influences.

Electronic thought forms resonate in the atmosphere through the use of television, cell phones, radio, and short waves. These are artificial means of transferring thought forms that have an unconscious effect on our thinking. Just as momentary images in a frame of film work on the mind subliminally, thought images that are broadcast through the air work on our unconscious mind. In turn, this has an influence on how we think, feel and react.

Mass thought by a nation, culture, or religion is another type of generated thought form, multiplying the energy of single thought forms by millions. Imagine if all the people of every nation of the world thought of each other as brothers and sisters. There would be no war or poverty. This may sound simplistic; yet if our thoughts emanated from love instead of hate, the world would experience peace. Throughout our history, mass thought forms have been extremely dangerous. The rise and fall of Nazism, Fascism, and Communism were possible because vast numbers of individuals thought the same way. Now terrorism is acting out on the world stage for the same reason.

We need to learn to protect ourselves from harmful thought forms. The thoughts of disincarnate souls who are bound to the earth can also influence the way a person in the physical body may think and feel. This is especially true if the person is of a weak mind and will. Many mass murderers once incarcerated begin to appear more normal; this may be because the disincarnated entity that once influenced their thinking has now fled to someone else, free and mobile to influence.5

Even the possessions around us hold thoughts of their previous owners. There is a story of a woman who every time she wore a specific piece of antique jewelry would fall seriously ill. Doctors were baffled by her condition. When she would not wear this particular piece of jewelry, she would feel better. This happened several times. Finally, her husband recognized what was happening to her. He took that piece of jewelry and buried it in his backyard. Her symptoms disappeared and she vowed never to buy another piece of pre-owned jewelry again.6

Old houses and antique furniture also hold thought forms of their previous owners in the same way. An old house holds all of the memories and thought forms of each individual soul who once lived there. People who are attracted to old homes probably lived in that era or even that house in one of their previous incarnations. Therefore, they take comfort in the thought forms the house emanates. Ghosts that are tied to earth, especially from suicide or murder, may reside in the house where they once lived. They find some comfort and clarity remaining near the home in which they resided.7

The point of understanding the nature of thought is to learn to let outside thoughts come and go and not be influenced by them. If we do not let thoughts come and go, we can become confused and emotionally disoriented. We will also lose the opportunity to develop our own creative will, mental faculties and spiritual intuition when we allow outside thoughts to influence us. Higher faculties, of our mental body and intuition can only develop if we discriminate between outside thoughts, innate thinking, and inner intuitive promptings. Through the spiritual understanding of the nature of thoughts, you can begin to elevate your consciousness and thereby create your own karmic destiny.

> *All that we are is the result of what we have thought: it is founded on our thoughts, it is made up of our thoughts. If a man speaks or acts with an evil thought, pain follows him, as the wheel follows the foot of the ox that draws the carriage.*
> *All that we are is the result of what we have thought: it is founded on our thoughts, it is made up of our thoughts. If a man speaks or acts with a pure thought, happiness follows him, like a shadow that never leaves him.8*

> *Gautama Buddha*

Chapter Reflections to Guide Your Spiritual Search

- Intuition comes from the depths of our own inner self and remains with us; it is not fleeting.

- To clear the pathway for intuitive thoughts to flow, ignore your anxious and hurried thoughts associated with the impressions in your mind.

- Everyday life should be guided by discrimination and inspired by the highest intuitions.9

- The Rosicrucians' believe that harmful thoughts and desires can be kept out of the mind by *"thought substitution."* Their theory is based on the principle that two thoughts cannot exist at the same time in the mind.

- If one has negative thoughts during the day, replace them quickly with something positive.

- Dr. Harry L. Kenmore would tell me to imagine myself wrapped in a cocoon of white light to protect myself from harmful thoughts and negative influences.

- *"A single grateful thought raised to heaven is the most perfect prayer."* Gotthold Ephraim Lessing

References

1.   Hall, Manly P. *Questions and Answers,* 30-31
2.   Khan, Inayat. *Spiritual Dimensions of Psychology,* 204
3.   Kalchuri, Bhau. *Lord Meher,* 3812

4. Peale, Norman Vincent. *The Power of Positive Thinking*, 167
5. Heindel, Max. *The Web of Destiny*, 26-38
6. Duce, Ivy O. *How A Master Works*, 693
7. Cannon, Dolores. *Between Death and Life*, 169-178
8. Buddha, Gautama
9. Baba, Meher. *Discourses*, 262

    *www.rosicrucians.com

11

Happiness and Suffering

o o o o o o o o o o o o o o o o o o o o o o o o
"It is felt that a disciplined mind leads to happiness and
an undisciplined mind leads to suffering, and in fact it is
said that bringing about discipline within one's mind is the
essence of the Buddha's teaching."

—*HH Dalai Lama* *

Happiness

*"Happiness and unhappiness are not like snow or wind; they can be
ruled and recognized according to the law of nature: unhappiness is
ignorance, and happiness is knowledge."*

—Paracelsus

Every person is seeking happiness in life. A mind that is happy is free from
anxiety and worry. Family, friends, career, intellectual, and spiritual pursuits
are all in balance. Our emotions are in harmony with our expectations. The
expectation of how our immediate world should behave is dependent on
three factors: first, your karmic plan (based upon your previous actions in

past lifetimes); second, personality development during this childhood; and third, free will in this life.

His Holiness Dalai Lama says self-discipline of the mind is the key to being happy in life. Psychiatrist, David D. Burns M.D., in his book, *Feeling Good: The New Mood Therapy,* reflects a similar approach to happiness. He says cognitive recognition of your own thoughts, perceptions, and expectations of others is an important step in understanding your own emotional state and applying self discipline to the mind. When you feel depressed, you are responding to an event or someone in your life that has not met your expectations.

Learning to use our spiritual intuition to identify our thoughts and expectations will enable us to discipline our mind and achieve a feeling of happiness. We need to evaluate, in a new way, how to respond to life's experiences. Our thoughts and feelings that determine our happiness depend on this new way of perceiving and interacting in life. In order to change our perceptions we need to understand the principle that underlies how our past is now manifesting in our daily experiences with family, friends, coworkers, and acquaintances. This principle is really an outcome of our karmic impressions. How we respond to each person and situation in the present is an outcome of a combination of this karma, our individual personality, current patterns of behavior and free will.

When we allow negative thoughts about our self, situations, and other people—whether karmically from the past life or new karma in the present life—to take residence in our minds, we develop feelings of inadequacy, anger, jealousy, and fear. Negative emotions and thoughts from past lives are released into our circulatory system from our emotional and mental seed atoms. This is how our karmic impressions reach our current brain and mental body.[1] We are given the opportunity in each life to overcome a dysfunctional pattern of thought by learning to use our spiritual intuition and self-discipline to replace negative emotions and thoughts with positive ones. To compound this problem, we may be in a current life family that fosters negativity. This will make it harder to work through emotional and mental roadblocks to achieve the happiness we deserve.

Cognitive therapy, Buddhist teaching, and positive thinking are wonderful guides for developing your self-discipline and a new perspective to change your past karmic patterns. Happiness can be achieved in your present life when your desires and thoughts are focused on your life's purpose. Finding the right path toward your life's purpose or goal depends on knowing what actions to take. Doing what makes you feel good just for the moment is a sure way to derail your happiness. Impulsive actions are quick fixes for immediate gratification. They are not grounded in intelligent discrimination and intuition to achieve long-range goals.

Materialism has become a means to achieve happiness in Western—minded societies. Life-styles of the rich and famous are dreams both young and old seek. It is difficult to keep what has true value in your heart and mind when those around you promote unrealistic goals.

Dr. Harry L. Kenmore described how he achieved happiness: by turning within himself and finding *"that happy little feeling inside." "We all have it. We are all born with it. We just do not develop it. It is the spark within us that we call God."* This is why one cannot find happiness in materialism, in people, objects, or even substances. Happiness does not last unless it comes from within, the God part of you that is the spark within every individual soul. This is what Dr. Kenmore meant by finding *"that happy little feeling inside."* Turn within yourself and think of God. Do not look for happiness outside yourself.

Awaken the spark of God inside of you. Find happiness in unselfish thoughts, desires, and actions. How you perceive the world will begin to change. You will no longer expect others and situations to create your happiness. By helping a fellow human being or a suffering animal, you will be developing new sources of happiness that will spring forth from within. Look for ways of doing things that will make the world a better place for your loved ones, friends and nature; then you will make others happy. The happiness of the God part of you will then come forth.

Suddenly, you will realize that what you originally considered happiness on earth is really a form of contentment manifesting from the God within. You do not need to rely on anything or anyone to make you happy. You are just content in being.

> *Our life might be much easier and simpler than we make it: the world might be a happier place than it is; there is no need of struggles, convulsions, and despairs, of the wringing of the hands and gnashing of the teeth; we miscreate our own evils. We interfere with nature.2*

Suffering

> *"Man does not seek suffering; but it comes to him as an inevitable outcome of the very manner in which he seeks happiness"*
> —Meher Baba **

All experiences in the physical world are dual in nature. At times we experience the pleasures of fulfilled desires but we also experience the pain of unfulfilled desires. Our individual soul needs to experience the opposites—pleasure and pain—in order to progress through the evolution of consciousness.

We cannot know happiness without knowing suffering, joy without pain or good without evil.3

When self-discipline of our emotions and mind are ignored, our individual soul is immersed in suffering. When we seek desires that are in conflict with our inner values and life's purpose, our path will lead us to disappointment. The energy behind these desires keeps growing. The un-fulfillment of the desires and increase of inner tension are the cause of our suffering.

Mental and physical suffering has its roots in our karma from previous lifetimes and from our actions due to free will in this lifetime. Of the two types of suffering, mental suffering is the worst. It is caused by deeper karmic impressions and is a more painful form of suffering to the soul than physical suffering.4 Specifically, depression is a physiological and emotional reaction to disturbing and overwhelming problems in life if the tendency is karmically present. Dysfunctional thinking can further escalate physiological disturbances, creating a vicious cycle of mental despair. Our genetic tendencies towards this type of mental suffering is due to our past karmic impressions of unresolved issues and can manifest in our current life if the environmental conditions are present.

When we are born with afflictions or they manifest early in life, we may be finishing up old karma from a past life. Afflictions that arise in our later life may be from our actions in the present life.5 When I was growing up, my family knew a man who was ruthless in business. He would not give an inch in showing a little compassion to others. His philosophy was *"business is business"*. By the end of his life, his ruthless treatment of others caught up with him and he became a very ill man. In the later part of his life when he needed compassion and support, his family and friends disassociated themselves from him. In his after-life experience, all of the cruel impressions brought on by his actions and experiences on earth will need to be relived and assimilated. The lesson of compassion will then become a part of his karmic record and, hopefully, in his next incarnation he will become a more compassionate individual to others.

As Edgar Cayce also reiterates in his writings, all suffering is due to previous actions of the soul. All illnesses are karmic in origin. In his over 14,000 life readings, he was able to help most people with their physical afflictions. He directed them to take specific remedies, practice deep prayer, forgiveness, and to search within for the cause of the affliction (from some action in a previous life). In some cases, only minor relief was possible due to the soul's karma being too great.6

Some physical illness is brought on as a way to humble our ego. Medical intervention may be able to alleviate some symptoms of the disease. A complete cure really does involve the person understanding why a particular organ or system is out of balance. The Rosicrucian fellowship link organ dysfunction with possible reasons why we are out of harmony with our expectations and life's purpose.

> *Is our heart causing us problems? How many times have we lost our tempers and raged like mad, putting tremendous strain on this part of the body? Or are other organs of our system weak and debilitated? We may be sure that, either in this life or a previous one, we have lived in a way that the effects find manifestation in our particular physical ailments. Otherwise we would not now be suffering, and the sooner we take the lesson to heart and commence to live a better life, more in harmony with the laws of nature we have broken, the sooner our suffering will cease.7*

Through intelligent use of self-discipline of the mind, we can face our karma from past lives. Buddhist teachings, positive thinking, and cognitive therapy are means at our disposal to perceive and change desires and expectations that prevent our happiness and cause suffering. When we take God as our *"constant companion"* we can find our *"happy little feeling inside"* and awaken our spiritual intuition.

Chapter Reflections to Guide Your Spiritual Search

- Self-discipline of the mind is a key factor in finding happiness.

- Cognitive therapy is a technique to identify your dysfunctional thought patterns.

- Replacement of dysfunctional thoughts with healthy ones will bring self-confidence into your life. If you make a mistake at work, do not think that you are worthless. Replace the thought of worthlessness with the thought that everyone makes a mistake, I will do better next time.8

- Live your life in moderation and you will not suffer the extremes of duality.

- Making others happy will automatically bring happiness to you.

- Real happiness can only come from within our inner self, not from influences outside our self.

- Suffering may be due to previous, negative actions of the soul. Accept the responsibility for the suffering. Coming to terms with why you are suffering will open up your heart to healing. An avenue of relief will present itself.

- Taking God as your *"constant companion"* will awaken that *"happy little feeling"* within you.

References

1. Chaney, Earlyne. *The Mystery of Death and Dying*, 19-21
2. Emerson, Ralph Waldo. *The Complete Writings of Ralph Waldo Emerson*, 167.
3. Baba, Meher. *Discourses*, 99-101
4. Baba, Meher. *Discourses*, 392-393
5. Woodward, Mary Ann. *Edgar Cayce's Story of Karma*, 45
6. Langley, Noel. *Edgar Cayce on Reincarnation*, 9-10
7. The Rosicrucian Fellowship. *The Heart: A Wonderful Organ.* phamplet
8. Burns, David D. M.D. *Feeling Good: The New Mood Therapy*, 51-74

*Lama, Dalai HH and Howard C. Cutler, MD. *The Art of Happiness—A Handbook for Living*, 32-3
**Baba, Meher. *Discourses*, 389

12

Sleep and Dream States of Consciousness

○ ○

"Clairvoyant observation bears abundant testimony to the fact that when a man falls into a deep slumber the higher principles in their astral vehicle* almost invariable withdraw from the body and hover in its immediate neighborhood. Indeed, it is the process of this withdrawal which we commonly call 'going to sleep'."

—*C. W. Leadbeater* **

When we fall asleep at night, it is because our physical body needs to recharge the primary life forces. We could say that the sleep-state of consciousness is an inescapable need. There can be no substitute for sleep. Although we can vary the hours to a certain degree, eventually our body and mind will succumb to sleep.

Scientists have concluded that prolonged sleep depravation will lead to bodily disorders, impairment, and derangement of our brain functions. The brain will deteriorate rapidly and we will begin to lose our alertness. Our mind will slowly be unable to solve the simplest problems of everyday life.

One night's lack of sleep is equivalent to a 25 percent loss of our conscious functions. Studies have also shown that excessive sleep lose over a long period of time will cause other parts of our body to deteriorate—sometimes with permanent results. From the spiritual perspective sound sleep provides us with the opportunity to return to our original unconscious state with God. When we are in a deep, sound sleep we are one with God, but unconsciously one.1

The individual soul in its natural state of existence is not the physical body. The physical form is the medium through which consciousness expresses itself. In our awake-state of consciousness, our soul's spirit bodies are confined into one space in and around our physical body. In the sleep-state of existence our spirit bodies are given a chance to escape every evening from this cramped and unnatural existence. Our subtle and mental bodies are able to experience a more natural state of freedom. Sleep gives the mind much needed rest from the physical body and the world's distractions.

An appropriate analogy to visualize this concept would be to imagine wearing an uncomfortable, restrictive suit of clothes all day. Upon returning home in the evening, we want to remove the confining suit, kick back, and relax. Well, it is the same way with our soul bodies during sleep. We unconsciously can leave our confining form and enjoy an evening of astral travel in the realm closest to earth.

When we enter the sleep or dream-state, our spirit bodies separate and rise up out of the physical body. The subtle and mental bodies leave the physical and etheric bodies behind to attend to the process of revitalization.2 In this state of existence, we have no conscious knowledge of our physical form. Although the link with the physical body remains intact, pleasure and pain are only experienced in the dream-state; the dreams remain real to the consciousness until the soul awakens to the physical world again.

When the individual soul's subtle and mental bodies emerge from the sleeping physical form, they hover only a few feet above in a cloud-like appearance. They retract back into the body when the awakened state of consciousness once more is dominant. The silver cord, bluish gray in color, is still tethered to the physical body. It is elastic in nature (made up of fine astral matter), similar to the consistency of a giant bungee cord, as described by clairvoyants. The silver cord is capable of stretching great distances.3 If the silver cord were to snap while sleeping, death would be immediate and swift. The death certificate would declare that the person died of natural causes. When a person dies in their sleep, due to old age or health complications, it may be considered a blessed death.

Whenever the individual soul goes into the deep sleep-state or unconsciousness due to either an accident or effects of anesthesia during an operation, the subtle and mental vehicles immediately withdraw to hover just above the physical body. This is the reason why people having a near-death experience during an operation say, they experienced floating above their body.4 The soul's spirit bodies can also leave the physical form temporarily in a coma state or as a result of excessive use of alcohol and drugs.5

An individual soul of spiritual advancement learns to travel further away from the body during the sleep-state, even to distant parts of the earth or solar system. One can even consciously recall the events of the experience during the night upon their awakening. Spiritually advanced souls also become helpers during their sleep-state in times of need, when natural catastrophic events occur or in times of crisis.6 Souls dying en masse from natural catastrophes, wars, and, in our present time, the collapse of the World Trade Towers, where a large number of individual souls perish all at once, are helped by advanced souls to cross over to the other side.7 The victim's conscious state is so disturbed by their sudden, shocking death that they are in need of special assistance by the helpers.

The spirit bodies of younger souls can only hover close to their physical form while in the sleep-state. Their consciousness is not spiritually developed to the point where they are aware of the possibility of traveling away from their physical form while they are asleep. As their consciousness progresses, they begin to perceive their true nature as a multiple-bodied individual. Once they realize their spiritual potential, they can join the hierarchy of spiritual helpers.

One can initiate this involvement by focusing one's thoughts on selfless service to others before falling asleep. Becoming a candidate for spiritual advancement also requires an understanding of the after-death experience. The consciousness withdrawn from the physical body is able to vividly see, hear and smell through the organs of the subtle body in the astral world.8 Some of the experiences encountered in the astral world may be frightening to an unprepared soul. Once you become a spiritual helper, you may begin to remember your experiences, but only symbolically rather than explicitly. As you continue to function in this realm, your physical brain vibrations will be altered to accept and understand the impressions gathered in this state.9 If this occurs, you may actually wake up with the conscious memory of your experiences. Spiritually advanced souls that are consciously able to astral travel great distances remember all of the events when they awaken to the full physical consciousness.

Time has no bearing on the astral plane of existence as it does in the physical world. This is why a dream can flash by one's consciousness in a matter of seconds.10 Dreams of people, places, or events which we do not recognize can be memories of past lives.11 Recurring nightmares of drowning, fire, explosions or crashes may be memories of events that happened in a past life of how we died. Similarly, we can have prophetic dreams of a future event.

C. W. Leadbeater in his book, *Dreams,* describes the five types of dream states that the soul can experience. The first is that of a true vision: The soul sees itself on a higher plane of nature, such as dreaming of heaven or dreaming of being in the presence of a revered religious figure. This will give the individual soul a great feeling of inspiration and happiness when returning to the awake-state.

The next type is the prophetic dream: In this case the soul can see or is told of some future event affecting loved ones or friends. The clarity and accuracy of the dream depends upon the soul's ability to translate this information to the awake-consciousness. Training is usually needed by the individual soul to develop the ability of this kind of recall.

The third type of dream-state is called the symbolic dream: Here the individual soul has experienced a diminished version of the prophetic dream-state. In this state, information comes through jumbled in the form of symbolic images rather than a clear train of thought. Each symbol represents some piece of information; but in the awake-state, the mind has to piece all of this together like a puzzle. Most people experience this type of dream.

The fourth dream-state is called the vivid and connected dream, or a *"remembrance dream"*: The individual soul has total, vivid recall of a sequence of events. This is triggered when the soul wanders away from the sleeping physical body and has an astral experience. The dream is vividly remembered in the highest detail in the awake-state with all the impressions of touch, sound, and visual sequences.

The last dream experience is the confused dream: This dream originates in the physical brain and is not associated with higher experiences. Sensual desires or fears usually trigger the chaotic dream. It becomes a dream of senseless, unintelligent images or events, usually occurring from a recent earthly event, which was stored in the unconscious memory of the physical brain.

When we sleep and dream at night, we are experiencing all of the associations with people, objects, and our environment as if we were in the awake-state. But all this exists and takes place within us. The experiences in the dream-state of sleep are our sanskaras interacting with each other in our unconscious mind. While the soul is in the dream-state of existence, the unconscious mind is wearing out old sanskaras and not creating new ones. So dreams can reduce our sankaric burden.12

We should not try to cheat the sleep process. Sleep is not only necessary for the proper functioning of our physical, mental, and spiritual health but also to give the spiritual bodies a respite from the cramped confines of the physical form. When we do not sleep, we do not get a *"soul-recharge"* and the health of our physical body and mind begins to deteriorate. Once recharged, the soul with the spirit bodies residing in the physical form feels refreshed and is able to face the problems of life in the days ahead. Loss of sleep will eventually catch up with us, especially in our later years, interfering with our physical, mental, emotional and spiritual health.

> *"Sleep is the means by which the mind withdraws temporarily from the pressure exerted by the age old load of impressions and desires. In sound sleep, consciousness becomes latent for the time being, until the burden of unspent sanskaras forces it to manifest again in the awake-state."*[13]

As Huston Smith stated, in his PBS interview with Bill Moyer, *The Wisdom of Faith,* it is when man is in a deep, dreamless state of sleep that the soul goes back to God in the beyond state of existence.

Chapter Reflections to Guide Your Spiritual Search

- When we are in a deep, sound sleep we are one with God, but unconsciously one.

- The lack of sleep causes the mind to deteriorate, resulting in a lack of memory, difficulty in concentration, depression, and irritability.

- Be discriminating with the music, movies, and television shows you choose to entertain yourself with before retiring for the night. The thought forms may disturb your sleep.

- Prayer or meditation before bedtime will attune you to your higher self in the sleep-state.

- Edgar Cayce stated that dreams have been given to man for his benefit. Interpreting our dreams and their symbolism can provide insight into our unconscious mind.

- If one wants to solve a problem or find something that is lost, present it to your higher self before going to sleep. The answer will present itself in the days to come either in a dream or as a thought upon waking.

- When you awake from your sleep, *"Attend to God while the world waits. Your first thoughts in the morning should be of God. Let the activities of the world come second."* Mani Irani

References

1. Baba, Meher. *Discourses,* 20-21
2. Leadbeater, C.W. *Dreams,* 20-24
3. Kaplan, Pascal. *Understanding Death from a Spiritual Perspective,* 5
4. Moody, Raymond. *Life After Life,* 34-55
5   Leadbeater. *The Inner Life,* 231-233
6. Leadbeater, C.W. *Dreams,* 52-54
7. Leadbeater, C.W. *The Life After Death,* 62-65
8. Duce, Ivy O. *What Am I Doing Here?,* 36
9. Leadbeater, C.W. *Dreams,* 44
10. Kaplan, Pascal. *Understanding Death from a Spiritual Perspective,* 25
11. Baba, Meher. *Meher Baba on Sleep,* 33-35
12. Baba, Meher. Ed. Don Stevens. *Listen Humanity,* 116-127
13. Baba, Meher. *Meher Baba on Sleep,* 15

*Astral vehicle refers to the subtle (emotional) and mental spirit bodies of the soul.
**Leadbeater, C.W. *Dreams,* 20

PART 4

Understanding Death from a Spiritual Perspective

13

Death, The Great Equalizer

o o o o o o o o o o o o o o o o o o o o o o o o o

"There is a secret to the art of dying. The soul faces the timeless moment of initiation into lifes most secret and sacred mystery. The light seeker will enter paradise. The average soul will enter the high astral. The dark soul will walk the lonesome valley of the judgment. But all will eventually evolve toward the heart of God."

—*Earlyne Chaney* *

People often think of death as the terminator but really it should be called the equalizer. At the time of death, the individual soul—whether rich or poor, black or white, Hindu or Christian—is suddenly separated from their best pal, the physical body. The surroundings and loved ones they were once so intimately involved with in this brief sojourn of life will disappear from sight. All that the individual soul has worked for and accumulated in the physical world is suddenly snatched from their grasp. Everything that the soul associated with as me and mine is gone. The connection with family, home, friends, possessions, and power, disappear, as well. The soul stripped of everything it once thought was the reason to live has been taken away by death. What happens next to the individual soul in the journey through the progression of life and death, according to Inayat Khan and Meher Baba, depends on how the soul lived its life.

Once the physical body is separated from the etheric, subtle, and mental bodies the spiritual significance of death to the worldly-minded soul, the spiritually inclined, and the evil-hearted individual becomes a different experience in the realms of the after-life. Each journey takes place in the plane of conscious existence the soul has prepared through thoughts, desires, and actions while on earth.

The Worldly Person

"For the worldly person—who views both his own death and the death of others as signifying the final and complete annihilation of consciousness and individuality—the phenomenon of death forces a confrontation with the issue of the meaning and significance of life itself."

—Pascal Kaplan **

When a worldly individual holds on to the grip of materialism in life too firmly because of constant thoughts and desires for self-centered pursuits, at the time of death it will be very difficult to let go of this life on earth. During their life, the worldly person neglected to develop a higher level of spiritual aspiration. The individual's thoughts and actions throughout life were primarily focused on material gain and status. This departed soul, with the ego consciousness, will use the time on this new level of existence trying to return to the physical world, instead of working with the spiritual guides to move ahead and review the just-departed life.

A worldly individual who is preoccupied with material attainments pushes aside all aspects of finding out about the death process during life. That individual relies on established religious beliefs and neglects to investigate what will happen when physical existence comes to an end. The fears of death formed in childhood remain unresolved. When the instantaneous moment of death approaches, the individual will probably miss the opportunity of grasping the *"Clear Light of the Void"*, God, because of anxieties, fears, and misconceptions about what lies ahead.

My father-in-law is a good example of someone who had great fears of dying. He faced death in his youth on the beaches of Normandy; but as he grew older, the fear of death increased. When his wife passed away in 1992, he lost himself in pursuits of the world. As his heart disease grew worse over the next several years, his fears of death were translated into extreme anxiety over living alone. He came to live with my wife and me after he experienced a second heart attack. At this point, we encouraged him to talk about his expectations of death. It was at this time that I was seriously researching and collaborating with my wife for material for this book.

One night at the dinner table, he related a Near Death Experience he had the night before. He saw himself standing outside of his sleeping body. He became so frightened that he had a hard time re-entering his physical body again. My wife and I felt this would be a *"teachable moment"* to share the after-death process with him. He basically did not want to hear what we had to say; and yet, he had no solid religious background to provide some comfort.

His health rapidly declined and other opportunities to alleviate his fears were not available. He spent his last days in a hospice reaching out to all available religious practitioners asking questions about what will happen to him when he dies. He would only accept the answers through his limited understanding. He never did ask us for more insight into our understanding of the death process. We continued to spend much time with him creating an atmosphere of peace and quiet. When he lapsed into his death coma, we remained calm to allow him to let go peacefully.

If you always thought that you, as an individual, would cease to exist after death, then when you actually die and continue to maintain your consciousness, you will be confused and overwhelmed in the after-life realm. You will not believe that you have actually died. A guide will try to approach you and convince you that you are indeed dead even to the extent of showing you your lifeless physical body lying in the mortuary. [1]

Inayat Khan discusses the need for parents to begin to educate an individual soul, as an infant to begin the spiritual education needed to prepare the soul for the life and death ahead.

> It is never too soon in the life of a child for it to receive education. The soul of an infant is like a photographic plate which has never been exposed before; and whatever impression falls on that photographic plate covers it; all other impressions which come afterwards have not that effect. Therefore, when the parents or guardians lose the opportunity of impressing an infant in its early childhood, they lose the greatest opportunity. [2]

The infant soul coming from the spirit realm brings with it the impressions of this angelic sphere, as well as its own sanskaras to be expressed in this life as its karma. But until the age of seven the infant is only receiving impressions from the parents, environment, and interactions with other people that will influence their later life.

If undesirable impressions have fallen upon an infant at that time, after-wards, whatever education you give, that first impression remains concrete and solid. Nothing can erase it afterwards.3

Kevin J. Todeschi in his book, *The Reincarnation of Famous People*, based on the Edgar Cayce readings, explains that effective parenting, according to spiritual intuition, can assist or inhibit a child's higher spiritual development. Edgar Cayce provides examples of souls who were famous in their previous life now reborn into the twentieth century to parents lacking the spiritual intuition necessary to guide and develop their purpose and potential in this incarnation. Even though we choose our parents for our needed experiences, it is the karma and responsibility of the parents, linked to their own purpose in life, to educate their child with respect to his or her true spirit nature.

Now, lets go back to the original discussion of what will happen to the worldly person upon death. Has the individual soul pursued and accomplished their purpose in this life? Has the soul pursued development of spiritual intuition? How will this impact their death experience and existence in the after-life?

A certain amount of happiness can be derived from material possessions within a balanced life of spiritual values. Moderation with all worldly things is an important key to living a life where spiritual advancement can take place and the progression of life and death is understood. When we become unbalanced and centered on the material side of life, sacrificing the spiritual side of ourselves, we will be unable to recognize ourselves as spirit when we enter the after-life at the time of death.

Harvey A. Green describes how the worldly person will experience death in the lower astral plane. When death occurs, consciousness is unchanged and no better off than when alive in the physical body. Now, while experiencing the world of thought, in the astral realm, with close proximity to the dense physical world of form, there exists a condition of false perception and confusion. The soul is unable to let go of the material world while existing in the outer edge of the astral world. The soul experiences a sense of unreality. The individual remains troubled and can even feel that they have lost their mind. This blurring of divisions between the physical and astral worlds as described by Harvey A. Green is tortuous to the soul.4

When we strive to fulfill our purpose in life, we should also develop our spiritual side to be prepared to enter the after-life. When we are children, we depend on our parents to lay down our spiritual foundation so we are prepared to face life and meet death with joy and without fear. If the opportunity for spiritual understanding was not developed as a child, as adults we need to take the responsibility now for our own spiritual growth. It is up to each of us to find our own path in life and discover the spiritual perspective of death.

The Spiritual Seeker

"A true aspirant neither seeks death nor fears it, and when death comes to him he converts it into a stepping stone to the higher life."

—Meher Baba ***

Bal Natu was a spiritual seeker all his life. His family raised him in India to believe in spiritual masters and advanced souls. He lived his life in constant companionship with God. A teacher in the Indian public school system, he was familiar with self-discipline; yet, he was always open to new ideas and technology.

He was a frail man needing medical interventions throughout his life. In his eighties, he was admitted to a hospital in Pune, India. There he was treated with the latest advanced medical procedures to prolong his life. Bal Natu was not interested in extending his life. His firm spiritual understanding of life and death allowed him to greet death with ease and welcome anticipation. So, when the doctors confirmed that he was entering the dying process, he was most relived to discontinue all treatment. He was sent home to die surrounded by loved ones and his favorite spiritual writings. He had a smile on his face when he died.

When spiritual aspiration has been awakened in an individual soul, attachment to the material and physical world gradually lessens, enabling the soul to recognize the special opportunity death has to offer. Aspiration for spiritual understanding can start at many levels. The best time to awaken spirituality is during childhood, as was the case with Bal Natu. However, it usually begins when a person experiences a tragic loss of a loved one or a traumatic experience that jolts their comfort zone. Current attitudes and beliefs are shaken and one begins to question, what is life and death? Suddenly, the norms and beliefs one was brought up with can no longer comfort or give answers to the questions that begin to arise deep within the soul. This turning point can cause a person voluntarily to search for spirituality and alter values and beliefs to come into balance with the yearnings of the inner soul.5 By aligning values with true morals backed, by pure and unselfish motives, one is beginning the spiritual search. This is called entering the spiritual path for the individual soul, or involution.

There are various stages of a spiritual seeker, from the beginner to the saintly aspirant. Each will face death according to their level of awakened spiritual consciousness. An individual may be a believer in God but practices religious rites and rituals unintelligently and mechanically, whereas the more advanced seeker is one who has forged their own inner path: through true inner contact with their higher self. This higher self is the unconscious part of God, the soul within everyone. There are as many paths to God as there are individual souls in creation. Each path is different and every soul must find his or her true path.

Advanced spiritual aspirants manifest their personal relationship with God outwardly by the unselfish and compassionate deeds they perform. Their uniqueness is their ability to be associated with a specific religious order but retain their own direct link to God. This is what we consciously should all strive for in order to achieve eventual liberation from the circle of life and death.

The after-death state for spiritually minded individuals manifests according to the religious thought forms that are anticipated upon death. One will begin the initial after-life journey according to one's religious inclinations about the after-life. For example, the initial phase of the after-life experience is the *"greeters"* at the end of the tunnel of light. They will appear to us as individuals that during our life we held most dear. The *"greeters"* can read our thoughts as we approach the portal of light; therefore, they appear to us as Christ, Buddha, Abraham, or other saintly figures and even loved ones, depending on the soul's religious beliefs. Through this interaction the soul will feel comfortable and can progress smoothly to the next level of the after-life.6

However, when we bring fears to our death experience, our thought-forms can be quite horrifying. In this case, we may be greeted by distorted figures from our imagination of what we anticipate the after-life to be. Some near-death experiences have been recorded that do not involve seeing a bright white light with a feeling of peace. These individuals should become aware that this experience was really due to their own thought forms and not a real experience of hell that they thought they would be experiencing after death.7

An explanation about the higher astral planes (the beginning of the spiritually minded soul's journey) after the initial death phase, is given by Lewis Spence.

> ...worries and cares of earth are all together absent, the insistence of lower desires has worn out in the lower divisions, and it is now possible to live continually in an environment of the loftiest thoughts and aspirations. The third division is said to correspond to the spiritualistic "summerland," where the inhabitants live in a world of their own creation—of the creation of their thoughts. Its cities and all their contents, scenery of life, are all formed by the influence of thought. The second division is what is properly looked on as heaven, and the inhabitants of different races, creeds, and beliefs, find it each according to his belief. Hence, instead of its being the place taught of by any particular religion, it is the region where each and every religion finds its own ideal.8

During life, we are given the opportunity to prepare ourselves to achieve the best and most joyous experience in the death phase of the progression of life and death. We do not need to abandon our present religion to become a spiritual seeker. Once we begin the journey on our path, spiritual intuition will unveil the original essence of our being, regardless of our religion; and we will be prepared to face death as a spiritual seeker.

The Evil Person

> *" But there are some people who are of such an evil nature that they enjoy a life spent in vice and degenerate practices, a brutal life, and who delight in giving pain."*
>
> —Max Heindel ****

In the world today, there is no shortage of evil souls—from drug dealers, murderers, terrorists, and all those in between. In my search to understand the consequences of living an evil life, I discovered that such souls would experience a most horrifying after-death existence according to the Universal Laws. In contrast to the spiritual and worldly individuals, the evil individual's departing consciousness with the subtle and mental bodies falls into a realm called the *"Outer Darkness"*. In Harvey A. Green's book, *Life and Death: The Pilgrimage of the Soul*, based on the readings of Edgar Cayce and Emmanuel Swedenborg, a detailed description of this realm is given. Cayce describes the outer darkness as a dimension that is *"void of hope, love, friendship, kindness, benevolence or any of what we have come to know as human qualities."*9

The life choices we make on earth are what draw our spirit to the realm we most resonate with in death. The Universal Law of Like Attracts Like is also in operation in the astral realm of the after-life. The lowest vibrational spirits are attracted to this existence in the after-life termed the *"outer darkness"*. In this realm, the pain and suffering that the evil soul experiences is a hundred-fold in intensity because there is no physical body acting as a circuit breaker or shield. The soul will perceive pain through the eyes and consciousness of the victims in the life just lived. The pain and suffering the individual soul experiences in this realm is through thought consciousness. When we are in the physical body and we experience intense pain, the body shuts down our consciousness, just like an electrical circuit breaker in a home will trip on overload. In the after-life, the consciousness of the individual soul experiences the pain more directly because the physical body is no longer there to act as this circuit breaker.

Individual seekers whose consciousness is of a higher level would see the astral being of these evil souls as sick and deformed, barely alive, exuding horrible emotions and vibrations. For those souls that go to the *"outer darkness"* there is no contact with others, only the feeling of total loneliness exists. For those who live near the center of this world, it is the darkness of the blackest black, causing terrific fear to its inhabitants.10 Imagine, being blind with no tactile feelings to establish your equilibrium or contact with another person. You are alone in a world of your own consciousness made up of your own evil thoughts.

As one moves closer to the outer edges of this world, the darkness appears gray, as if one were in a fog. Terrible odors of decay and stench fill the heavy air. The dwellers of this world look angry and menacing, shabbily dressed and run down. The dwellings of these inhabitants are in the same condition. The feeling and smell of evil is everywhere. There is no friendships or alliances amongst these dwellers; *"Tormenting one another would be the natural state of relationships."* 11

It is not possible for souls to live for all eternity even in the outer darkness because even odious, evil individuals have a hope of redemption. *"Again, outer darkness is not a punishment, rather it is the ultimate manifestation of our own undoing, and He who is Mercy would never abandon us to such spiritual agony."* 12

The impressions such evil ones have acquired and spent in their past earthly life require extreme measures to help them begin to gather new impressions in their consciousness—human qualities of kindness, goodness and compassion.13 So, the outer darkness is a starting point for such souls on their way to redemption. On earth, such evildoers are very difficult to help turn towards their better impressions. There is always in front of them the tantalizing world where their lust, greed, and anger can become entangled. It is only in the subjective state of the outer darkness of the after-life that forces of change can be exercised to help bring the evil impressions to a halt and to slowly plant a seed of love and compassion in their consciousness.

Chapter Reflections to Guide Your Spiritual Search

- Evaluate your current aspirations in your life using your spiritual intuition.

- Societal norms are not always in tune with spiritual values.

- Moderation with all worldly things is an important key to live a life of spiritual advancement.

- Dedicate all thoughts, words, and deeds to God, then your true purpose for this lifetime will advance naturally.

- Awaken your spiritual intuition to the unifying thread in the oneness of all religions.

- Ask God for guidance and the quiet voice within will guide you.

- It is never too late on earth for an evil doer to avoid the realm of the outer darkness after death. Even one who begins to turn towards good thoughts, words, and deeds may avoid the worst of this realm.

- Acknowledging the wrongs done on earth through retrospection within your higher self can be very helpful to expend the emotional energy that is at the root of evil impressions.

- Small steps begin with substituting negative thoughts with positive thoughts. This *"replacement"* leads to positive desires and actions.

References

1. Cannon, Dolores. *Between Death and Life*, 19-26
2. Khan, Inayat. *Education*, 1
3. Khan, Inayat. *Education*, 2
4. Green, Harvey A. *Life and Death: The Pilgrimage of the Soul*, 80-84
5. Kaplan, Pascal M. *Understanding Death from a Spiritual Perspective*, 42-45
6. Cannon, Dolores. *Between Death and Life*, 19-26
7. Chaney, Earlyne. *The Mystery of Death and Dying*, 74-77
8. Spence, Lewis. *Encyclopedia of Occultism*, 42
9. Green, Harvey A. *Life and Death: The Pilgrimage of the Soul*, 84
10. Green, Harvey A. *Life and Death: The Pilgrimage of the Soul*, 83-90
11. Green, Harvey A. *Life and Death: The Pilgrimage of the Soul*, 87
12. Green, Harvey A. *Life and Death: The Pilgrimage of the Soul*, 89
13. Cannon, Dolores. *Between Death and Life*, 122-123

* Chaney, Earlyne. *The Mystery of Death and Dying*, Preface
** Kaplan, Pascal M. *Understanding Death from a Spiritual Perspective*, 41
*** Kaplan, Pascal M. *Understanding Death from a Spiritual Perspective*, 47
**** Heindel, Max. *The Web of Destiny*, 32-33

14

Six Types of Death

o o o o o o o o o o o o o o o o o o o o o o o o o
" Death is not dying of the self, or the ceasing of the spirit, or
even the ceasing of the purpose of the spirit; it is rather life,
with mind, soul, and understanding departing from a worn
out garment or a house no longer fit for its inhabitant."

—Manly P. Hall *

When viewing the process of the individual human soul entering the physical
world, we accept the fact that there is only one way and that is through the
process of birth. But when the individual soul leaves the physical world, there
are several possibilities of how death will occur. Each type of death will cause
the soul to experience a different type of existence in the initial phase of the
after-life. Ultimately, all types of death will terminate the individual soul's
conscious connection with the physical body and its life force. The physical
body will cease to function and the organs will shut down. This is the clinical
death of the physical body.

The soul consciousness survives the death of the physical body and enters
the after-life. This after-life state of existence is not a physical or geographical
place; it is a world created by thought forms in another dimension of
consciousness. The same Universal Laws are operating in this dimension of

existence in the same way they operate throughout creation. The experience of each type of death will impart a different psychological impact on the consciousness of the individual human soul as it is dying.

The first type of death most individuals will experience is the normal death—dying from a disease or old age. The second type is accidental death when death may occur before its natural time most likely due to carelessness. Next is death by murder, which is the destruction of the physical body by another human being. Death by capital punishment is the premature demise of an individual, according to the laws of society, as a consequence of the wanton destruction of another human being. Death by suicide is the ending of the individual soul's physical existence by one's own hand. Finally, circumstantial death occurs on a massive scale involving war or natural catastrophes.

Normal Death

The majority of human beings on earth will die a normal death due to natural causes. Young or old, each will have lived their contracted life span, representing their karma and sanskaras. Every soul designates their time of death, with a guardian angel, prior to birth. The time of death coincides with the soul's life plan. The life plan includes designs for obstacles to be overcome through relationships, the pursuit of talents, and the development of spiritual aspirations. Once the specific life plan is completed, the individual soul will die.

It is easier to accept the death of an elderly person because that person would have had the chance to live a full life than to accept the death of babies, children, or teenagers who die from the same diseases. However, a seemingly shortened life span may in fact be just what the individual soul needed in this lifetime to experience, according to their planned karma.

There are many karmic conditions for why an individual soul needed to die young. One condition might be to finish up leftover experiences from a previous lifetime, especially if they died an accidental death, or the family needed to experience the loss of a child. Sometimes, it is because the soul sees ahead that this incarnation will not be of karmic benefit for what it needs to accomplish in this lifetime.[1]

In either case, young or old, the individual soul does become aware that death is approaching. As the disease progresses, the bonds between the physical and both the subtle and mental bodies begin to loosen. The individual soul actually begins to turn towards death as a release from its suffering. It is at this time that the soul should be using the remainder of life to prepare for the best death experience. Young or old, this type of death is the best way to enter the after-life and gain the most spiritual benefits.

When an individual soul dies a normal death in their sleep-state, it is an easier death. While asleep, the soul, within the subtle and mental bodies, is already hovering a few feet above the physical form. Therefore, if death comes at that moment the subtle and mental bodies can be more easily released. The individual soul will then progress in the after-life according to a normal death. When you die a normal death you are in a better state of mind, at the moment of death, to reach out for the first *"Clear Light of the Void"*, God.

Accidental Death

Accidents are the second most-common cause of death. Accidental death is an unnatural state of dying. Death can happen so quickly that the individual soul is sometimes unaware that he or she has departed from their physical body. According to Harvey A. Green, souls will appear to be going mad when those around them, still on earth, are not paying attention to their pleas for help. This type of death may further upset the soul if it sees its body destroyed or in pieces. The soul may perceive the astral body it now inhabits also in pieces. This occurs because the astral world is made up of one's own thoughts. Until the soul becomes accustomed to the new state of existence, thoughts will resonate with the recently detached physical world. The time the soul will remain in this condition depends on the predestined time death was to occur. Once the contracted time is reached, the soul will progress as in a normal death. In some cases the soul needs to return to the earth quickly to continue to live a life according to the remaining sanskaras—usually the individual soul will then die a young death.

Accidents in which individuals do not die can be looked upon as a tapping on the shoulder by a guardian angel. An accident might occur when one strays from their contracted life's purpose. The accident can be considered as a wake-up call to get back on track. A near-death experience might be such a wake up call.

Most accidents occur due to some form of carelessness when an individual is not giving their full conscious attention to what they are doing. So many people today rush around trying to accomplish too many things in one short span of time. Mary Summer Rain in her book, *Phoenix Rising*, describes why accidents are occurring more frequently and will increase in the near future.

> *Plane crashes would occur from a mechanic's oversight during his routine maintenance checkup, or from a captain's miscalculation or from an air traffic controller's fatigue. Train derailments would occur from a switchman's error, or from a sleepy engineer, or from a section of track bed left in disrepair. Buses, automobiles, motorcycles, subways, and bicycles were all included within No-Eyes' framework of the unnecessary fatalities caused by the freak accidents.*

And what amazed us was the fact that all of these disasters could be avoided if the people involved would simply take the extra time to be more aware. It was a sad and avoidable aspect of the Phoenix Days, yet because people need to hurry through their daily lives, it was to be a certain reality. 2

By stilling the mind and listening to our inner voice, intuition can protect us from accidents. This inner voice of intuition will cause us to question our actions, "Should I take the next flight, stay home from work or go in late because I have an uneasy feeling?" This is not abnormal. I remember the story of a World Trade Center worker who called in sick on September 11, 2001, because she had an uneasy feeling that day and did not feel she should go into work. There are other stories of individuals arriving late to work that day at the World Trade Center because of certain uncontrollable circumstances or delayed departures from home. These souls may have unconsciously been responding to their inner intuition. This is not to suggest that everyone should stay home from work on a whim. But by becoming more cautious when you perceive a strong, persistent, uneasy feeling about a situation, you might avoid unnecessary suffering.

Accidents can also happen because of an imbalance in the rhythm of your life. When you pursue the things that go against your life's purpose and spiritual development, you may get a tap on the shoulder to tell you to change course or slow down. When you develop your spiritual intuition, you will be in a better position to determine the actions to take on any given day. Norman Vincent Peale tells us not to be *"timid in the face of life."* We should not run away from our responsibilities for fear of impending doom. Facing life's challenges and overcoming obstacles are a part of why we return to the earth time and time again. But as we slow down and become more silent within, our intuition will help us to make the right decisions in life and avoid suffering.

Murder

A person who is murdered by another human being because of lust, greed, jealousy, or anger has had their karmic destiny cut short, through no fault of their own or possibly as a karmic repayment of a debt for a murder they committed in a previous lifetime. They are in the same position in their immediate after-life state as that of an individual soul who has prematurely died in an accident. However, the murdered victim overcome with the shock of separation from the physical body becomes preoccupied in seeking revenge from the murderer in the after-life.

Murdered souls will cling to the physical world as they enter the astral plane. Not realizing they have died, they try to contact loved ones. Initially confused from the quick and violent nature of their physical death, the souls now gradually become aware of the unjust circumstances that caused their demise. Now filled with revenge, they cannot turn forward and go into the after-life.

Guardians trying to bring the souls away from the physical world have difficulty. They try to calm the souls and may even intervene to put things right for their family. If they did not have a plan to care for their family in the event of death, it would contribute to their state of turmoil. If a murdered individual was a single parent, she or he might be held to the earth plane because of concern for the children, especially if a written will was not left.

A murdered individual will need to live out the preordained life in the astral world because their life was cut short and the karmic sanskaras need to be spent before entering the after-life and progressing. If the individual murdered soul was a spiritual seeker, the guardians can help ease this time by putting the consciousness of the soul into a *"semi-sleep"* state to complete the destined life span. C.W. Leadbeater clarifies what occurs at the time of a premature death.

> *Those victims of sudden death whose earth-lives have been pure and noble have no affinity for this plane, and so the time of their sojourn upon it is passed, to quote from an early letter on this subject, either in "happy igno-rance and full oblivion, or in a state of quiet slumber.... On the other hand, if men's earth-lives have been low and brutal, selfish and sensual, they will be conscious to the fullest extent in this undesirable region."* 3

Capital Punishment

Over the last two decades, capital punishment has been extensively debated. From a spiritual perspective, is capital punishment the most appropriate method to punish an individual for a brutal murder of another human being? In place of capital punishment, individuals believing in one life would rather replace capital punishment with life incarceration. Taking a life is just not acceptable to them. On the other hand, families of murder victims expect justice in terms of capital punishment to balance the brutality of the offense.

From a spiritual perspective, it is better to execute a true murderer as humanely as possible. Spiritually, the best method of execution is hanging by the neck.4 It is the taking of the breath that will cause death and release the soul from the physical world. Just as the soul takes a breath at birth in order to enter the physical world the breath is taken away at the time of death.

Karmically, if a murderer is executed as punishment for the crime, the soul will then progress with a clean slate of balanced karma. Although the soul will still spend time in the hell-state of existence, the karmic debt will be paid and succeeding lives on earth can proceed according to other karmic needs. However, if the murderer is incarcerated and allowed to progress to a normal death, then the after-life will be treated as the death of an evil person. They will not only spend time in the hell-state but will have to experience being killed in another incarnation. Usually, this will occur while he or she is in the prime of life. Their life may be cut short due to an accidental shooting during a robbery or being mistaken for an animal by a hunter while in the woods.5

People who protest the death penalty are concerned that the wrongly accused will die for a crime they did not commit. From a karmic prospective, an individual soul wrongly put to death, albeit terrible, might have in a previous lifetime committed a murder and framed someone else for that crime. In this lifetime, the law of karma may be balancing the debt. 6 However, the justice system is spiritually responsible and held accountable for correct identification of murder suspects. Prosecutors and defense attorneys should know that they would be held karmically responsible for consciously withholding any evidence that convicts the wrong individual to death.

Suicide

Manly P. Hall in his book, *Reincarnation: The Cycle of Necessity,* describes suicide as *"an action of self-will against the self."*7 Suicide is committed with the expectation of ending all pain and misery. Individual souls falsely believe they will attain peace through nonexistence. Manly P. Hall continues to tell us that there is no gain for committing suicide, only consequences according to Universal Laws.

> *The average modern who resorts to suicide is impelled either by a boredom with physical life or by the fear of the consequences of action. In both cases the security, which is sought beyond the grave fails utterly, and only bad karma results. The most usual karmic result of suicide is that a future personality will die under conditions where the desire for life will be the greatest. There is no escape from insufficiency except self-improvement.8*

When a soul commits suicide, the whole course of their planned life and the lives of family and friends is disrupted. In other words, a hole is created in a planned universe. What the suicide does not realize is that they will still have to face and solve the problems that they originally tried desperately to escape. In a future incarnation, the suicide will need to return to earth to face the burdens they tried to escape from, in addition to other new life challenges. When a person commits suicide, they believe it will take away their pain, that death is the answer when pain becomes unbearable. Understanding that suicide will not provide an end to pain but actually creates more karma and intense bindings to the problems that seemed insurmountable can assist one to avoid this most unfortunate type of death. *"Man cannot escape his responsibilities, but he is never given more than he can bear although often he is tested to the utmost."*9

After one has committed suicide, the soul realizes too late what it has done. Right after the act, the soul suddenly wants to get back into the physical body it terminated and it cannot. It finds itself in a nowhere's land, a land of limbo, not really dead and yet not really alive. This state of existence is referred to by Edgar Cayce as, *"in-betweens"* or *"halfways"* by Manly P. Hall. Ancient civilizations termed suicides the *"undead."* The soul cannot progress forward, as in normal death, or go back into the body, as in the case of a near-death experience. The individual no longer has a physical body to interact with or spend sanskaras.

After death, the suicide begins to feel the suffering and sorrow he or she has caused to the loved ones left behind. Feelings of despair and loneliness are overwhelming. They find themselves residing in a place of darkness and cold, of confusion filled with lost souls that cannot associate with one another. Here souls linger in the low astral realm close to the physical earth with other souls who are unable to move on in the after-life phase of existence.

A soul must remain in this state at least until the time of one's planned earthly existence was scheduled to end. Suppose an individual was destined to live until the age of seventy-two but commits suicide at the age of twenty-two. Because of their planned unspent sanskaras for this lifetime, they will exist in this state of suffering for at least fifty earth years.

Meher Baba divides suicide into four groupings: lowest, low, high, and highest. The lowest form of suicide is when individual souls end their life due to selfish motives based on lust, greed, or anger. An example might be of a person who has murdered someone and, rather than face the consequences of their action, commits suicide. Teenagers with emotions running high might take an overdose of alcohol or drugs because they are unable to cope with the pressures of their life. Someone who has lost everything and is in financial ruin might dive off a rooftop to end their suffering.

The low form of suicide occurs when a soul has disgust for life due to ill health (Euthanasia) or poverty. They are usually old but want to end their life sooner than their allotted time. After death, they will spend the normal three-four days in their life review state. Once the link is severed with the physical world, this soul will enter the hell-state of existence until all of their negative sanskaras are spent. Unlike the souls of the lowest form of suicide, who may spend hundreds of years semi-attached to the physical world, their hell will be in a close alignment with the physical world. They will be tantalized with the fulfillment of worldly desires that cannot be fulfilled.

The third type or high form of suicide is based on higher motives and self sacrifice for the well being of others. This is a death of strong beliefs, higher motives, and values. The soldier who jumps on a mine or hand grenade to save his fellow soldiers does so with unselfish motives. One who dies of starvation for a cause they believe will help their fellow man also belongs in this category. The Christians who died in the arenas of the Coliseum in Rome because of their strong belief in the Christ were acting from a high spiritual level.

Individuals that commit a high form of suicide will spend the usual three to four days of life review. Due to their spiritually motivated actions, they will be allowed to spend time in the heaven-state of existence until it is time to reincarnate. Because of this selfless act, the individual soul will gain spiritually in their journey, sometimes eliminating several incarnations.

The last and highest class of suicide is committed by those souls who have a burning desire to reunite with God.

> *If and when a suicide is embraced purely for the sake of attaining God, it can have the effect of achieving liberation or Mukti. The masters have always warned aspirants against resorting to suicide in the intensity of their longing for union with God, for there is too great a room for self-deception and inadvertent admixture of inferior unconscious motivation.10*

Suicide bombers believe they are acting in accordance with God's will, but are they acting through their limited egos and taking innocent lives with them? Their motive, it seems, is grounded in a cultural and social indoctrination rather then from a true longing to be united with God. They are usually aware that their families will receive monetary rewards because of their actions. Their zeal is to destroy themselves and all those around them. They are not only destroying themselves but are murdering other individual souls at the same time. Because of their motives and actions, they will exist in the astral realm or enter the realm of the *"outer darkness."* In addition to a most unfortunate after-life, such individuals will need to spend many lifetimes experiencing the effects and suffering they caused to their victims.

For those souls who commit horrific crimes and will not relent to the spiritual helpers, there is an alternate result apart from existing in the *"outer darkness."* Their soul and consciousness can be terminated and become nonexistent. Their substance becomes part of the unconsciousness of the universe. Their separate ego personality must be destroyed. There will be no hell of suffering, just nonexistence. This is so rare a reaction in the universal scheme it is hardly referenced. An individual soul must be so far off the evolutionary path that re-absorption of the individual soul benefits the universe as a whole.

Once absorbed, the soul's individuality is eternally lost, the soul no longer exists as a life force with a destiny of its own, and this is the "banishment" referred to in the Judeo-Christian texts. This is also touched upon in the Cayce discourses when he said, "the individuality of the soul that separates itself is lost". (826-8).11

Suicide should never be thought of as a part of one's karma. It is an aspect of free will. Even though many people are brought up knowing that suicide is unacceptable in their religion, when they are faced with an overwhelming surge of desperate emotions, all reason is lost. But, if you are brought up learning about the true nature of the soul in life and the aspects of the after-life in death, you may have the strength to keep a firm grip on your emotions during a crisis.

Suicides in some future lifetime will have a great fear of death. Such individuals will have a strong will to live and will try to cheat death to avoid facing the same horrors experienced when they committed suicide in the last life. Unconsciously, their ego-mind will be repulsed at the aspect of death. There is still a life of karmic payback for a soul who has committed suicide. In one of their next lives, the suicide may be born into a lifestyle with everything to live for—a wonderful marital relationship, great kids, plenty of money, a promising career. Then, suddenly and violently, their life is ended. The karmic repayment may occur as a plane crash, car accident, burst aneurism, or a victim of violent murder.

If we understand, from the spiritual perspective, that we must face our karma now in this lifetime or we will meet it again in a future existence, suddenly everything appears in a different light. If one does not allow suffering to play out to the end, then one has to finish it in another incarnation. As we progress spiritually, we also realize that there is assistance available to us on earth through family, friends and organizations. When we face our suffering, the Law of Grace sends the help we need to find strength and even peace in any time of crisis.

Circumstantial Death

Circumstantial death is *"being in the wrong place at the wrong time."* This type of death usually occurs on a massive scale but can also affect an individual. In circumstantial death, the individual soul is exposed to extreme conditions of danger. For example, when nations go to war, individuals are drafted into the military and exposed to battle. By accepting their national responsibility, they find themselves in harm's way in circumstances beyond their control. In times of war, a soldier in this situation will not incur karma when killing the enemy because it is not an act of premeditated murder.

If a soldier is fighting with the understanding and belief that their actions are aligned with national security, then they will not be held karmically responsible for following orders to kill the enemy.12

Circumstantial death may also occur to individuals living in an unstable area of the earth, prone to earthquakes, volcanoes or flooding. In either case, the individuals facing this kind of death may approach the after-life as in the case of premature, accidental death. With this magnitude of destruction and loss of life, God in His great mercy dispatches scores of *"helpers"* to assist the confused souls to advance normally through their death process in the after-life.

Death occurring by karmic association is another aspect of circumstantial death involving free will. In this case, an individual will be in the proximity of a large group or crowd, such as an airplane, cruise ship, or stadium. The overwhelming karma of the other individual souls, whose lives are about to end, is in control of the outcome of the situation. The unfortunate individuals whose time to die has not yet come are in the wrong place at the wrong time. But the destructive incident may consume them all, if the possibility is there, to die before their time. Yet many times we hear stories involving plane crash survivors who miraculously escape death.

I have presented the six different ways that death can terminate our spirit connection to the physical body. The way in which we will experience the after-life phase depends to a large extent on how we die. Dying a normal death gives us the greatest opportunity to merge with the *"Clear Light,"* God. However, our karma, free will, and ignoring our intuitive inner voice may cause us to experience one of the other types of death. The important point in this chapter is to develop a spiritual understanding of the death process to avoid the suffering that accompanies the other five death experiences. When you experience death in any form, consciously strive to a higher sphere in the after-life by remaining calm and avoiding the influence of negative thought forms from the just-finished life. Know that there will be an ending to any uncomfortable experience and that assistance from the spiritual helpers is right there at all times.

Chapter Reflections to Guide Your Spiritual Search

- When death is approaching, turn within to your higher self. Intuitive thoughts will quietly and calmly enter your consciousness.

- Let your loved one know it is all right to die and move on, and that you and the family will be okay.

- Provide all medical interventions that will not cause the individual soul to face insurmountable suffering when dying.

- When the soul is approaching the death phase, heroic life-saving techniques may cause suffering. The individual soul is being released from the physical body naturally. Bringing the soul back into the dying body artificially can prolong their suffering.

- By listening to your inner voice of intuition, you can avoid unnecessary suffering from a premature death.

- When the individual soul dies of an accidental death or murder, the consciousness remains confused for a period of time.

- Through prayer to God, you can help ease the anguish and revenge of a murdered victim. Let the victim know, through your thoughts and words, that you are okay and want them to progress forward.

- When an individual soul commits suicide, it severely disrupts their spiritual growth. Suicide is never a solution.

- No one in life is given more then they can handle according to the Law of Karma. Obstacles that appeared do-able at the stage of planning with our guardian angel, prior to rebirth, may become overwhelming when faced on earth.

- How to help the individual soul who has committed suicide:

  - Send thoughts of hope, encouragement, and love.

  - Tell your loved one to seek out their guardians for guidance.

  - To console the individual, do the things they loved: reading their favorite books of inspiration, playing music, talking about their hobbies, sports, and pets.

  - Ask God to intervene to comfort and guide your loved one. God can hear your heartfelt prayer and will respond by sending His messengers to help.

References

1. Cayce, Edgar. *Discourses*, no.1648-2, 480-37
2. Rain, Mary Summer. *Phoenix Rising*, 155
3. Leadbeater. C.W. *The Astral Plane*, 75
4. Maharaj, Upasni. *The Talks of Sadguru Upasni-Baba Maharaja.*
5. Duce, Ivy O. *What Am I Doing Here?*, 23

6. Maharaj, Upasni. *The Talks of Sadguru Upasni-Baba Maharaja.*
7. Hall, Manly P. *Reincarnation: The Cycle of Necessity,* 169
8. Hall, Manly P. *Reincarnation: The Cycle of Necessity,* 170
9. Hall, Manly P. *Death To Rebirth,* 13
10. Baba, Meher. *The Advancing Stream of Life,* 118
11. Green, Harvey A. *Life and Death: The Pilgrimage of the Soul,* 120
12. Baba, Meher. *Meher Baba on War,* 156

    *Hall, Manly. *Questions and Answers,* 88

15

Preparing for Death and the Clear Light

o o o o o o o o o o o o o o o o o o o o o o o o o o o

"Yesterday, early in the morning, I obtained my freedom from all sorrow, and in the darkness of the night I got the purity of Eternal Life in my ego less state. He gave me my Real Individuality, and I got purity from the wine in the cup of illumination. What a glorious night it was and what a blessed morning when I received the pass for the highest- when I saw the Beloved and got mad and bewildered with Love. I was given the knowledge of beginning and end."

—*Hafiz* *

Every individual soul has a built-in cosmic time clock. You actually determined your time of death with your guardian angel before you were born. How does your body know when it is time to die? The heart-seed atom releases a death hormone into the blood stream when the time of death is approaching. This hormone is the trigger mechanism to begin the release of the etheric, subtle, and mental bodies from the physical form. 1

To be ready for this moment of death, the right attitude is needed. To develop this right attitude takes a lifetime of preparation beginning in childhood. Parents can begin to teach their children that death is not the ending of their life. It is just a beginning of a transitional phase between life and the next life. Through stories and answers to their questions, children can be guided to understand that death is as natural as going to sleep. This will not only alleviate anxiety about death but, as children grow up, they will open their consciousness to their true spirit nature.

When this opportunity to understand the nature of death is missed as a child, as an adult, you still have time to learn about the significance of death from a spiritual perspective. You can take the mystery out of death by reading books about the death process. The insights and direct experiences of the clairvoyants and advanced souls will be especially useful to explore the meaning of the moment of death and what to expect.

The initial stage in the death process, when the separation of the four bodies occurs, is the same for every soul, regardless of what type of death you experience, except for the suicide. When the etheric, subtle, and mental bodies separate from the physical form, your impressions, through thought forms, will be projected to create your initial experience in the after-life transitional phase. Whether you will see the grim reaper of death or the angel of light depends on your own conscious thought forms created by your beliefs about death. Since the after-life is manifested as a world of thought, it is not a world of physical substance. Whether real or not, here lies the confusion. You are in control of the projection you will see, through your conscious and unconscious thoughts.

While this process of *"letting go of life"* is taking place, loved ones looking on view the physical body as it experiences the death coma. At this point, contrary to traditional belief, the individual soul does not feel physical pain.2 The two soul bodies, (the subtle and mental), which carry away the consciousness of the soul personality, are experiencing the release of the burdens of the physical form.

In the normal death this separation brings an initial feeling of happiness. Each soul continues to feel this joy, depending on the positive accumulated impressions from this just-completed lifetime and the level of anxiety and fear about the approaching death.

Earlyne Chaney in her book, *The Mystery of Death and Dying*, outlines the death process from a practical spiritual point of view.

- Every individual soul in creation, prepared or not, will face the death process.

- Just before death is initiated, we have a unique opportunity to face God, in all His Love and Glory. This is called the *"Clear Light of the Void,"* which appears prior to the moment of death. *"The Clear Light is the gateway to salvation, and initiation, and liberation—the opportunity for deathbed salvation."* 3

- It is a once in a lifetime chance for *"liberation from one's karma."* But it is usually missed because we have not been educated during life to anticipate it. We might miss the *"Clear Light"* due to the fears we have about death from our instilled childhood religious beliefs.

- Missing this opportunity is a great loss because the individual soul will have to go through the cycle of birth and death for the next chance to grasp the *"Clear Light."*

As discussed in the chapter, "Six Types of Death," suicides, as a consequence of murdering themselves, miss the opportunity of the "Clear Light" completely at the end of their life. Even when they are allowed to leave the astral plane to progress through the process of the after-life, they will not have a chance to merge with the Light because they have prematurely cut their life short by their own hand. They must wait until another cycle of birth and death repeats itself to grasp *"The Clear Light"* at their next death.

Observing loved ones during their death process I noted how distracted they become as they prepare to leave all of their worldly attainments, family, and friends behind. Through my own spiritual search, I have learned how to assist a loved one as death approaches. Certain precautions should be understood and practiced. A special vigil around the deathbed should be one of quietude. At the moment of death, assist loved ones to focus their thoughts on God and the approaching *"Clear Light of the Void."* Even if the individual is in a coma, their consciousness is still connected to the body, hearing and seeing everything that is happening in the room.

If the dying soul lived a life where spiritual development was their primary focus, concentrating on God at the moment of death will come naturally. As the *"Clear Light"* appears, reunion with God, the Divine Creator, approaches. The vibrational level of the individual soul will resonate with that of God. As in the Universal Law of Like Begets Like, the final attraction and merging can be consummated.

There are many practices from various ancient esoteric, philosophical, and religious teachings, which will assist the individual soul to reach the needed vibrational level. *The Tibetan Book of the Dead* and *The Egyptian Book of the Dead* are two good sources from which to read at the deathbed. They provide a sequence of steps, which include special words that create the appropriate atmosphere. It does not matter which religious books are read from, as long as they provide a comforting and harmonious atmosphere coinciding with the natural inclination of the departing soul. Repeating any name of God, said with heartfelt love, has the power to draw one's consciousness to this higher vibrational level. 4,5

Many people who do not understand reincarnation expect to be united with God, *"The Clear Light,"* in a place called heaven for all eternity. Heaven, referred to in Christian theology, is really the final liberation of the individual soul from all the rounds of births and deaths—easterners call this Mukti. If one were really ready for God's greeting, Liberation, through the appearance of the *"Clear Light,"* countless lifetimes would have been spent in preparation to develop purity in their love for God. Whether you believe in reincarnation or not, the merging with the *"Clear Light"* will occur when your vibrational level is attuned and resonates with the energy of God.

Chapter Reflections to Guide Your Spiritual Search

- Prepare a will to provide for your loved ones so your focus at the time of death will not be on worldly affairs.

- Write a living will to prevent the administering of extreme life-saving techniques to interfere with your death process.

- Pain medications should not be taken that will render you unconscious at the time of your death.

- Quietude is most important around a dying person so they can focus on meeting the *"Clear Light,"* God.

- Do not discuss how you will divide your loved one's estate by their death-bed; they can still hear you.

- Dying at home in loving surroundings, if possible, will help a loved one reduce anxieties and feel comfortable as death approaches. Hospice services are an excellent resource.

- It is best not to interfere with the death process by euthanasia. Let the individual soul complete their karma naturally until the end. A program of medications can alleviate pain yet keep the individual conscious and focused on God.

References

1. Chaney, Earlyne. *The Mystery of Death and Dying,* 49-50
2. Chaney, Earlyne. *The Mystery of Death and Dying,* 44

3. Chaney, Earlyne. *The Mystery of Death and Dying*, 43-45
4. Khan, Inayat. *The Purpose of Life*, 33-37
5. Green, Harvey A. *Life and Death: The Pilgrimage of the Soul*, 77-78

*Hafiz, Shamsuddin Muhammad: A fourteenth century Sufi Perfect Master and poet of Shiraz. Died ca. 1389 A.D.

16

Death of the Physical Body and the Continuation of the Soul

"In a similar fashion, your physical form becomes the womb from which the spirit-soul must escape at the time of death, at the time of the soul's return to the higher sphere-for death is truly a second birth."

—*Earlyne Chaney* *

We need not be afraid of the spirit-soul's initial physical separation at the moment of death. It is as natural as the birth process. Dolores Cannon in her book, *Between Death and Life,* describes the physical separation process as natural and painless.

> *At one moment you're in one plane of existence and you blink your eyes, so to speak and you're in another plane of existence. That's about the physical sensation you have, and it's as painless as that. Any pain you feel in the process is from physical damage, but spiritually there is no pain.1*

It takes three to four days for the soul and the spirit bodies to completely leave the physical form. Until the final separation occurs, your soul is still attached to your form by the silver cord. You are freed, as St. Paul describes, *"in a twinkling of an eye."* This is so short a time in comparison to the soul entering the body at birth and maturing into an infant in nine months. In addition, the process for each of the three soul bodies to be complete in their development, during their maturation after birth, takes a total of twenty- one years. Yet, we are invited to wonder at the *"miracle"* of death as the soul is released from the physical body *"in a twinkling of an eye."*

Individuals describe leaving their body during a near-death experience as suddenly having a feeling of great joy, a release from all burdens. It is as if someone removed a heavy suit of clothes. Once the initial fears are overcome, there is eventually, a feeling of timelessness and great clarity for the soul. The type of death the soul endures influences this initial emotional and mental experience as the silver cord is severed.

How does the individual soul with the three spirit bodies leave the physical form at the time of death and continue with the same consciousness? Many clairvoyant and spiritually advanced teachers describe the beauty and mystery in the dying process.

Let us begin with all three permanent seed atoms that are finely attached to the soul bodies. They are impressed with the record of all the memories and experiences of who you are from your past lifetimes to the present, through evolution and reincarnation. The three atoms come into each new physical body at birth and leave with our soul at the time of each death. Many people are familiar with the Akashic Records or the Book of Life.

> *They are your soul's Book of Life, or your Book of Judgement, containing your personal Akashic Record. They embody within themselves the seed pattern of the individual soul, just as an acorn ensouls within itself all that will become an oak tree. Everything that you have done, said, or thought is recorded in the seed atoms of your own being. 2*

The emotional (astral) seed atom, which refers to the subtle body, has all of the qualities of your emotional weaknesses and strengths gathered throughout your soul's evolutionary lives. The important point is that this seed atom functions to *"reflect your present emotion"* from the pool of your past emotions. It is directly linked to the blood stream from its subtle position in the solar plexus and interacts with the glandular system of the physical body.3 This is how karmic impressions (sanskaras) return with you in every incarnation manifesting your spirit nature into the physical world.

The mental seed atom holds the record of all your mental thoughts from the beginning of your soul's human evolutionary journey. The images of past thought patterns, particularly of the last four incarnations, circulate in the blood stream, influencing what you think in the present life. Similar to the emotional seed atom, you can change your mind patterns through will power, prayer, and Grace once you become aware of the origin of your thoughts and feelings.

The heart seed atom, situated in the area of the heart, carries with it all of the karmic information from your entire evolutionary past, and continues to record every thought, emotion, and action in your present life.4 A detailed record of every aspect of your life just lived will be played back at death as your life review. Since this is a difficult concept to grasp I am including a quote from Earlyne Chaney's book, *The Mystery of Death and Dying*, where she answers the question of free will and the role of the three seed atoms.

> *The question is often asked, "Are we puppets of fate and karmic destiny, or are we free souls with the power to choose our own fate and destiny?" The enigma has long perplexed the seeker. The answer is found in the knowledge of these three seed atoms. The heart seed atom, containing its perpetual record of your past, ties you to your karmic destiny, while the mental and astral (emotional) seed atoms, containing the characteristic powers or weaknesses, enable you to control your future, your own destiny. Thus you have two seed atoms subject to your free will and a destiny of your own choosing—and you have one seed atom securely holding you to your karmic past destiny and "fate."5*

Your spirit through your heart seed atom, at the time of your approaching death, alerts your physical body to release a death hormone.6 This process of separation can proceed at a pace coinciding with the time it will take for the physical organs to die. All other types of death, besides the normal death, will progress at a much faster pace. When a person is instantaneously killed during an accident or murder, the organs will cease to function in an instant. The consciousness of the individual soul is unprepared for the unexpected change in his existence.

During the normal death sequence, the heart seed atom releases images of your impending death into the bloodstream. As these images enter the glands, the necessary glands begin to release their own set of hormones, which signals the higher spirit to begin the separation process from the lower physical form. As the death hormone flows into the nervous system, the sensations of pain are gradually dulled. This is important to note because many physicians prescribe pain-killing medication that will also numb your consciousness. One should try to remain conscious during the dying process to have the opportunity to grasp God's Light.

As the death hormone is circulating through the circulatory system, we can begin to observe, on the physical level, the withdrawal of the *"etheric or vital energies"* from the body. Vital physical organs begin to lose their function. As the life force withdraws, the feet will begin to grow cold and turn blue.

This life force gradually moves up through the spinal column to the head. This signals the silver cord to begin to fray and loosen its connection with the physical form.

Once the physical organs cease to function, the individual soul is now in a position to exit through the top of the head of the physical body. The three permanent seed atoms are preparing to withdraw through the silver cord. At this point, all pain stops. The mental and heart seed atoms still remain in the physical form while the astral (emotional) seed atom enters the newly formed astral body. The dying person appears to be in a coma that might only last a moment. Suddenly, the third eye opens (located in the center of the forehead), allowing the person to see visions of angelic spirits, beautiful scenery, loved ones who have passed on or revered religious figures. This is the moment one begins to see the dawning of the *"Clear Light."* One may arouse from consciousness to say goodbye to loved ones near the deathbed.7

This arousal from what appears to be the coma-state indicates that the mental seed atom is being freed from the body. The heart seed atom will leave the physical body when the newly forming astral body is complete, which usually requires three to four days. At no time during this period should embalming, autopsy, removal of organs for transplant, or cremation take place; the heart seed atom might be slow to depart. This will also disrupt the pictures of the life review, which are being transmitted. This waiting period should be observed for all types of death.8

When the heart seed atom finally departs, the silver cord breaks away from the body. Annie Besant provides us with an excellent description of this process through the eyes of a clairvoyant.

> *The process of withdrawal has been watched by clairvoyants, and definitely described. Thus Andrew Jackson Davis, "the Poughkeepsie Seer," describes how he himself watched this escape of the ethereal (astral), body and he states that the magnetic cord (silver cord), did not break for some thirty-six hours after apparent death. Others have described in similar terms, how they saw a faint violet mist rise from the dying body, gradually condensing into a figure which was the counterpart of the expiring person, and attached to that person by a glistening thread.9*

As previously described, for those individual souls who die other than a normal death, the process by which the death hormone is released and the seed atoms leaving the body may happen instantly and simultaneously. This is the reason why the soul is in a state of great confusion after death, believing they are still alive. The helpers in the after-life need to convince the soul that they have gone through the transition of death. Once the soul accepts that they are truly dead, they begin to proceed as if in a normal death. One should remember that this convincing process by the helpers can take days, weeks, or even many years for the departed soul to come to the realization that they have truly died.10

In the case of a near-death experience the separation process of the individual soul's subtle and mental bodies begin to be released due to some great shock or trauma to the physical body. However, for karmic reasons or for the soul's need to complete this lifetime, the soul is returned to the body. In many cases, people report seeing spiritual guides who explain why they have to return. Some may need to return to finish raising a child, complete a life's purpose, or prevent a loved one's grief. If this death occurred prematurely, there would be a gap in the planned continuity of this lifetime.

At times, a person wanting to remain on the earth plane convinces the spiritual guides that they are doing good work for humanity. Persons creating suffering for others may need to return to impart a positive influence in the world. In any case, when the individual soul returns to the body, the death hormone is no longer released into the blood stream and slowly dissipates, keeping the silver cord in tact.

The Secondary Light at the time of death is the second chance that the individual soul with positive impressions (who has strived during this life towards good deeds) has to enter the realms of the higher astral plane. The Light will appear to the individual soul one half-hour after the clinical death of the physical body.11 It is our own thought forms, dwelling on the threshold, which could prevent us from entering the Secondary Light, and thus the higher spheres in the after-life. At the time of death, whether we merge with the Clear Light, enter the Secondary Light or remain in the astral plane, Dolores Cannon assures us that we are never alone.

> *After dying, there seems to be a period of confusion for some spirits. All do not experience this. Much of it depends upon the manner of death, whether it was natural or sudden and unexpected. The main thing I found is the assurance that one is never alone after going through the death experience.12*

Death and the physical separation process are as natural as birth. The release of the three seed atoms from our physical body as the second birth assures us that our personality, consciousness, and spirit will survive. Physicians, spiritual counselors, and loved ones can assist the dying soul to have the best death experience when they understand the spiritual nature of the death process in all its complexities.

Chapter Reflections to Guide Your Spiritual Search

- Strive to live a life in preparation to merge with the Light of God.

- Become aware of your thoughts and feelings, knowing that through will power, prayer, and God's Grace, you can change your karmic impressions in your mental and emotional seed atoms.

- One should remain conscious during the dying process to have the opportunity to grasp God's Light.

- Prepare, during life, to merge with the *"Clear Light"* at death by visualizing yourself in constant companionship with God. This practice can also protect you daily from negative outside thoughts and assist you to automatically focus on the Divine Source at the time of death.

References

1. Cannon, Dolores. *Between Death and Life*, 15
2. Chaney, Earlyne. *The Mystery of Death and Dying*, 13
3. Chaney, Earlyne. *The Mystery of Death and Dying*, 13-16
4. Heindel, Max. *The Rosicrucian Christianity Lectures*, 79
5. Chaney, Earlyne. *The Mystery of Death and Dying*, 21
6. Chaney, Earlyne. *The Mystery of Death and Dying*, 49-50, 54
7. Chaney, Earlyne. *The Mystery of Death and Dying*, 55-56
8. Heindel, Max. *Occult Principles of Health and Healing*, 222
9. Besant, Annie. *Death and After*, 16-17
10. Heindel, Max. *Occult Principles of Health and Healing*, 228
11. Chaney, Earlyne. *The Mystery of Death and Dying*, 59, 63-67
12. Cannon, Dolores. *Between Death and Life*, 19

    *Chaney, Earlyne. *The Mystery of Death and Dying*, 54

17

Heaven and Hell

○ ○
"Hell and heaven are states of mind; they should not be looked upon as being places; and though subjectively they mean a great deal to the individualized soul, they are both illusions within the greater illusion of the phenomenal world."

—*Meher Baba* *

As the spirit bodies separate from the lifeless physical form, a life review is ready to begin. With the help of a guardian angel, the individual soul reviews the just-completed life backwards, like a film, from the death moment to the time of birth. This process is necessary for the soul to understand the consequences of their actions on earth and how well their life purpose was achieved. In other words, the soul consciousness views the effects of their actions in the physical world and the karma that was balanced or created.

When the life review is finished, the worldly, spiritual, and evil person will experience the heaven or hell state of consciousness in the after-life. Each experience is dependent on their individual thoughts and actions brought within the spirit bodies from the just-completed life. The type of death the soul experienced will also be a factor affecting their initial, subjective perception in the astral world. This assumes that the soul did not merge with the *"Clear Light of the Void"* at the moment of death.

Inayat Khan, in *The Soul, Whence and Whither*, describes the conditions each individual soul now faces in the astral world of subjectivity.

> *What will be the atmosphere of the world? It will be the echo of the same atmosphere which one has created in this. If one has learned while on earth to create joy and happiness for oneself and for others, in the other world that joy and happiness surrounds one; and if one has sown the seeds of poison while on earth, the fruits of these one must reap there; that is where one sees justice as the nature of life.1*

In order for the individual soul to assimilate the experiences from his earthly life, a more intense type of review needs to take place. This subjective intense review is called the heaven and hell states of consciousness. The rewards and punishments associated with the familiar Christian belief of heaven and hell is not an accurate understanding, according to esoteric and spiritual teachings. Heaven and hell are not physical or geographical places but states of consciousness in the astral world.2 The soul turns inward to experience the heaven or hell consciousness, as if it was a projected hologram within the mind. Without the heaven or hell state, the individual soul could not experience, analyze, and evaluate past earthly experiences. The soul would never make advancements nor be able to modify the ego-mind and make spiritual progress.

Meher Baba has given this description of assimilation of earthly experiences in the heaven and hell states of consciousness.

> *Thus the hell-state and the heaven-state become instrumental in the assimilation of experience acquired in the earthly phase, and the individualized soul can start its next incarnation in the physical body with all the advantage of digested experience. The lessons learned by the soul through such stocktaking and reflection are confirmed in the mental body by the power of their magnified suffering or happiness. They become, for the next incarnation, an integral part of the intuitive make-up of active consciousness, without in any way involving detailed revival of the individual events of the previous incarnation. The truths absorbed by the mind in the life after death become in the next incarnation a part of the inborn wisdom.3*

Many people wonder how an individual can experience the hell-or heaven-state through consciousness. You will experience the suffering and pain that you caused to others within your own thought consciousness at a heightened intensity because you do not have a physical body to act as a buffer for the pain or joy. In the astral world, you function through your subtle body (which is composed of energy and emotions), and the mental body (which houses the mind). It is through your subtle body that you will directly experience all the impressions of your past life. You are actually experiencing the pain and joy you have created for others on earth. Earlyne Chaney, in *The Mystery of Death and Dying*, has a clear explanation for the experiences of the hell-state:

> *To the soul in hell, the drama of the past life plays over and over again. The scenes of the soul's crimes unreel constantly before the memory vision. If you committed premeditated murder, you cannot escape the constant replay of the event, even to hearing the screams of your victims. Even though you may feel no remorse in the beginning of this hell experience, the perpetual "memory" of the deed, or deeds, eventually causes incomparable suffering.4*

Another aspect of suffering in the hell-state involves the soul's intense cravings and obsessive desires brought from the life just lived. Imagine extreme cravings for alcohol, tobacco, drugs, food, or sex without the physical body to satisfy them. The repetitive thought of these cravings cannot be satisfied through thought alone, because the cravings are of the coarse physical vibrational level rather than the surrounding astral world. Only through the physical body can coarse lower desires be gratified.

In the heaven-state, an individual soul will relive all of the good impressions created while on earth in the physical body. Through the subtle body, one can experience extreme joy, happiness, and bliss. If a person has pursued the more refined and higher vibrational desires while in life (such as music, poetry, and art that coincide with the vibrational tones of the higher spheres), they can then satisfy the desire for these experiences simply by the thought of it. The subtle organs of sight, hearing, and smell provide the consciousness access to experience this finer vibrational level. The individual soul will have these experiences with a heightened feeling of joy and happiness.

In many cases after experiencing the heaven-state, a soul can cast off the subtle body, leaving it behind. The soul begins to draw itself more into its own subjective state of consciousness, linked only to their mental body experiencing a higher state of existence. This is called the *"second death."*5 Here in the higher heaven divisions of consciousness, one can create one's own heaven-state of existence by tapping into the record of all past- life experiences. Through the mind of their mental body, one can recreate surroundings that correspond to any past earth incarnation. In this higher realm of thought consciousness, one can experience the companionship of loved ones in settings of beautiful gardens with lush greenery, lakes, and exotic birds. It is as real to the soul as if one were alive on the earth plane. In this realm of the higher heavens, the souls of the hierarchy of God assist one to advance spiritually and experience the beauty of harmony and love. The higher heaven experience may last for hundreds of earth years.

Just as there is a higher heaven division of consciousness, there is also the lower spectrum of the hell-state. At the moment of death, a soul with a majority of extreme evil tendencies enters this astral realm of death, the *"outer darkness"*; first introduced in chapter 13. This is the extreme hell-state of experience, which is, in this case, an actual realm of existence. This lower region of the outer darkness was created as a reaction to souls with extreme negative sanskaras and activities. But even this region is not a punishment. Those agonized souls will eventually experience a benefit through the universal laws operating in the outer darkness. Harvey A. Green provides us with a chilling account of the nature of this horrific realm. This is the hell-state also described by Helen Greaves and Emmanuel Swedenborg.

> *It is so dark in the realm of outer darkness that the dark hurts and panic rips us without our knowing why. Like our material universe, outer darkness seems endless and without any meaningful boundaries. There is nowhere we can go to escape the agony and horror which fills almost every part of our being, and the desire to flee consumes us.* 6

Because the life of these souls were filled with horrible thoughts, motives, and deeds, the usual life review, which is a time to reflect and understand the past life in a subjective mode, had to be modified to gain the soul's attention. Even in such an extreme hell-state of existence, there is the hope of redemption from sanskaric patterns of evil. As discussed before, the outer darkness is the result of a soul's choices and karma. It is not a 'punishment' given by God. Through the Law of Grace, God shows His mercy and love when the tortured soul begins to open his inner eyes to the angels of hope.

The terrifying experiences of hell that are depicted in late-Gothic paintings in the fourteenth and fifteenth centuries and the bliss of the heaven-state are both necessary stages in the initial death-state existence for the worldly and evil individuals. The spiritual souls who can either enter liberation or the higher heaven-state have prepared themselves over many lifetimes to deserve their reward. Those souls dying prematurely from murders, suicides and in many cases accidents, cannot begin their after-death process. They hover close to the material world in the astral realm until their predetermined death age is reached and their allotted sanskaras are spent slowly in the astral realm. But then, they too will go forward to experience the hell-or heaven-state. So, we are all destined, after we complete each lifetime to reap the consequences or rewards for our actions in life. This is part of the spiritual justice system according to the Universal Laws.

Chapter Reflections to Guide Your Spiritual Search

- The predominance of positive or negative sanskaras at the time of death will determine whether you experience the heaven-or-hell-state.

- The heaven-or-hell-state is not a permanent condition. When the experience is complete, the individual soul will be released to reap the higher heavens or reincarnate again.

- Negative sanskaras can be overcome when a sincere individual soul makes up his or her mind to live a more selfless and pure life.

- Accept the consequences if you experience the hell-state in the after-life, knowing it will not last forever. You will have a chance to do better in another incarnation.

- You prepare yourself for the experience of the heaven-state by learning to control your coarser desires in life.

- The assimilation of the experiences from your earthly life, intensified in the heaven-or-hell-state, will be stored in your mental body as wisdom for your next incarnation.

References

1. Khan, Inayat. *The Soul Whence and Wither,* 165-166
2. Baba, Meher. *Discourses,* 307-312
3. Baba, Meher. *Discourses,* 311-312
4. Chaney, Earlyne. *The Mystery of Death and Dying,* 129
5. Besant, Annie. *Death and After,* 67-76
6. Green, Harvey A. *Life and Death: The Pilgrimage of the Soul,* 89

   *Baba, Meher. *The Advancing Stream of Life,* 53

18

Caring for the Dead

○ ○
"When it is known that the end has come for some loved member of the family, this circumstance requires a wise and gentle behavior of those present at the occasion. The transition should be as peaceful as the nature of the ailment will permit. We should depart from this world as one traveling to a distant land, with the memory of those about us wishing us well and encouraging us on this life's supreme adventure. Though perhaps we have lived in confusion, it is good to die in peace."

—Manly P. Hall *

How does caring for the dead affect the departing individual soul? Death is the moment we anticipate all of our life, although we are not consciously aware of it. This is the most important moment of our life. This moment is more important than when we were born, the moment of marriage, birth of the first child, or owning our first home. This is the moment when our soul once again has the chance to gain true freedom from the circle of life and death. How we treat the physical body of the deceased can interfere with their reaction to the first *"Clear Light"* at the very instant of death.

As death approaches, the best scenario would be to die at home surrounded and comforted by the people and possessions one loved and cared about during life. When dying at home is not possible and the dying person must remain in a hospital, loved ones should make every attempt to spend time at their bedside to ease their apprehensions. While at your loved ones bedside, distractions and loud conversations should be kept to a minimum. Talking with others in the room should be done quietly. Discussions about how to divide your loved one's possessions should not take place in their presence. They can hear your conversations even while in a coma.1

Words of encouragement to your loved one will reduce fears of letting go of life. Reassure them that everyone they are leaving behind will be all right. Hysterical behavior and crying will only cause grief to the dying person and bind the soul to the earth realm for a longer time. The feelings emanating from your emotions will cause your loved one to feel tied to the family and their needs, interfering with their own passage into the after-life.2

Everything should be done to assist the dying person focus and grasp that first *"Clear Light"*, God, just at the instant of death. The dying person should be fully conscious for that final moment. Pain-killing drugs should not be used, if possible, that would render the dying individual unconscious at the time of death.

Just prior to the pronouncement of death, the vital energy passing through the etheric body stops flowing into the physical form. As death proceeds, the lower extremities and the feet are the first parts of the body to become cold. The life force is now moving up the spinal column to the head. Eventually, our soul and spirit bodies will exit through the top of the head.3

Once a physician has made the pronouncement that death has occurred, the individual's body should be left to lie in state for a time. The family should communicate with a mortician to remove the body and keep it refrigerated for at least three to four days before any embalming or cutting is done. If you live in a tropical country where such refrigeration facilities are unavailable, adjust to the situation, keeping the interests of the living and dead in mind. Health codes may have to be worked with to achieve the best caring practices for the dead.

One needs to remember that during this three-to-four-day period, the individual soul is still attached to the physical body and, at the same time, the new astral body is being formed to house the spirit bodies which are departing via the silver cord. This cord is attached to the top of the head of the deceased. Eventually, within a few days, to a clairvoyant, a perfect image can be seen of the deceased person floating just above the dead form. Individuals with less clairvoyance see it as a bluish gray cloud.4

Another reason we should wait the three to four days is because the heart-seed atom of the deceased is still being transferred to the newly formed astral body. All of the information of this life has been added to the soul's whole evolutionary record and stored in the heart-seed atom. During this transference process, the soul goes through its life review, whereby it sees its whole life played back like a film.

During this review period an autopsy, organ transplant, embalming, or cremation of the body will cause the individual soul to feel pain, as described in the works of C. W. Leadbeater and Max Heindel. This pain will not be felt in terms of physical pain to the body but pain in terms of thought through the subtle and mental bodies that are leaving the physical form (just as one feels discomfort in a bad dream while they are asleep). This disruption can even terminate the life review process because the silver cord may be still attached.

Spiritually advanced souls leave their body quicker than the more materially minded. The subtle and mental bodies are able to enter their new astral form with the seed atoms well before the waiting period. Once the silver cord has snapped, the spiritual bodies are no longer tied to the physical form and the three seed atoms have been transferred. Any physical mutilation at this time will not interfere with the life review.

Transplants present a serious problem for departing souls. Since time is of the essence, organs for transplant need to be removed immediately upon death or, in some cases, when the body is still functioning but is declared brain dead by a physician. Organ donations are such a noble deed, as it keeps someone else's loved one alive. Everyone should come to terms with this dilemma prior to his or her death. One's wishes should be written in a living will. There are forms available from the Rosicrucian Fellowship for this purpose.

Max Heindel, in the *Web of Life,* tells a story about man who brings his deceased son to an undertaker for embalming. After leaving his son with the undertaker that evening, he has a dream about him. His son appears to him in extreme pain, his mouth all distorted and bloody. The next day the man approaches the undertaker to see his son's body. Much to his horror all of his back teeth are missing probably pulled out for the gold fillings!

The time of spiritual death (separation of the individual soul and the spirit bodies from the physical body) varies for each individual. Therefore, the precautionary rest period of three to four days before any procedures are performed on the deceased is advised to prevent the individual soul from experiencing any shock, pain, or disruption of the life review.

We should not have any regrets if we have fulfilled death-wish promises to our departed loved ones to the best of our ability. How the body is disposed of after the three-to-four- day interval does not impact the soul's existence after death. In India, Zoroastrians bring the dead to a Tower of Silence where it will be consumed by vultures and other birds of prey. In the Jewish Orthodox culture, the body is buried before sundown on the day of death in a plain, unadorned coffin without embalming the body. In Tibet, after the three-to-four-day waiting period, the deceased is prepared for disposal by special people who hack the body into parts, which are then taken to a mountain and feasted on by wild animals. The belief being that the physical remains of the body assists other living beings to continue their existence.

In other parts of India and the world, cremation is widely accepted. Burning the dead is believed to return the body to its natural element very quickly. The ashes are then spread in various places loved by the deceased. It is believed that the Buddha was cremated and his ashes spread throughout places in India. When considering cremation the question to ask should be; will the departed soul become distraught as it views the procedures from the astral world?

Although the wishes of the deceased should be respected, there are times when family members of different faiths and beliefs question the instructions of their loved one. In such cases, what the departed soul believed and desired to be carried out should be respected if it coincides with the procedures which will enable the soul to achieve the best after-life experience. The ones who depart from this world enter into a spiritual after-life that is beyond and unaffected by the influence of religious sects and beliefs. As Manly P. Hall stated:

> "Funeral services, therefore, are an opportunity to express esteem and respect, and should have the simplicity and dignity appropriate to the occasion. Details of the funeral should be determined by good taste and the means available, but should always be modest and moderate."5

Many people leave instructions for the disposition of their remains either in a will or their last words before dying. These instructions should be followed within reason, especially if funds are limited. Plan a funeral within your budget. Be careful not to fall prey to funeral directors or representatives trying to make money at the expense of the bereaved family. At this emotional time, funeral representatives appeal to your sense of duty by saying, this is what your loved one would have wanted. Relatives who pass on will not benefit in the after-life from expensive funerals. If there is no objection, after the three-to- four-day period, the dead can be cremated, providing the least expensive way to dispose of the mortal remains. A clear spiritual understanding of the death process can help you to make proper funeral decisions.

Lying in state as an ancient practice of keeping the body undisturbed continues to reflect the spiritual understanding of caring for the dead. The underlying reason for this practice, is to allow the soul quiet time to form the new astral body and review the just departed life. After this brief period of time, various cultural and religious practices can be preformed for burial or disposal of the body that will not interfere with the spiritual progress of the deceased.

Chapter Reflections to Guide Your Spiritual Search

- When death is near, assist your loved one to relax and remain focused on God as the *"Clear Light of the Void"* approaches.

- What our thoughts are just at the moment of death is where we will be drawn in the after-life.

- Try to refrain from hysterical crying in the presence of the departed soul. Your loved one can still feel your emotions and become distraught in your suffering.

- Performing physical procedures on the dead body prior to the waiting period of three to four days can interfere with the soul's transition into death.

- During the three-to-four-day period, allow the dead to remain in a quiet place.

- We can express our feelings for our deceased loved one with flowers placed by their picture as a memorial. By this gesture they can see and feel that they were loved.6

- As Kahlil Gibran once said, *"Our sorrow over the dead may be a sort of jealousy."*7

References

1. Chaney, Earlyne. *The Mystery of Death and Dying*, 52-53
2. Kaplan, Pascal M. *Understanding Death from a Spiritual Perspective*, 65-66
3. Chaney, Earlyne. *The Mystery of Death and Dying*, 54-55
4. Leadbeater, C.W. *The Astral Plane*, 40-41
5. Hall, Manly P. *Questions and Answers*, 111
6. Kaplan, Pascal M. *Understanding Death from a Spiritual Perspective*, 65-67
7. Gibran, Kahlil. *The Kahlil Gibran Reader*, 47

    *Hall, Manly P. *Questions and Answers*, 109

Part 5

The Propelling Force of Love in the Circle of Life and Death

19

Seeing Our Loved Ones Again

◆

There Is No Death

o o o o o o o o o o o o o o o o o o o o o o o o o

"They are not dead.
They have but passed
Beyond the mists that blind us here
Into the new and larger life
Of that serener sphere."

—*John McCreery* *

People ask the question, will I see my loved ones again? Individuals believing in the one life, feel assured that they will see their loved ones again, most likely in heaven; but this is not necessarily the case. I have learned that we do see our loved ones again after their death, but not in the same way they once were.

For example, when we sleep and leave our physical body temporarily, we can reunite with a loved one for a brief time, if they are still in the astral world and have not reincarnated. It is a joyous time when our spirit bodies can reunite again. We will return to our sleeping body when our sanskaras wake us in the morning—our built in alarm clock! But our loved ones will continue to make their progress in the after-life. After spending time with them, we awake with a feeling of joy with the thought of them, since we do not always retain a conscious memory of our meeting.1

We may also continue to see our loved ones when they come into our lives again through reincarnation. This is due to The Universal Law of Attraction. The Law states that consciously or unconsciously, we are attracted to those individual souls of similar vibrational levels. We continue to meet with one another time after time.

Initially, when we die, our astral form is a replication of the physical form we embodied while on earth, only now it is composed of finer astral matter. But as we advance to the higher realms of pure thought forms and light, we no longer retain the same astral representation of what we looked like on earth. So, when we meet and greet each other at this level of existence, we recognize each other not as mother, father, brother, sister, husband or wife, but as truly good friends. We are drawn together in the after-life spheres through our mutual vibrational level and love.2 When the karma with a loved one is complete our vibrational attraction will end.

There is neutrality of gender in the astral world, but gender difference is necessary for our experiences on earth. Latent within each individual soul are the male and female impressions that find their expression through the psyche with only one gender dominant during each lifetime on earth. Male or female impressions are chosen to work out the karmic sanskaras for that specific lifetime. The gender that is dominant aligns itself with the corresponding impressions of the incarnated physical form.3,4 Gender misalignment or the balancing out of impressions is the cause of confusion that homosexuals confront during their life.5

Reports of near-death experiences describe encounters with figures illuminated by light at the end of a long, dark tunnel. This bright light, sometimes called the secondary light, reveals loved ones and religious figures to the individual.6 Such figures might have been a mother, father or spouse who have already passed on into the after-life. Many also recall seeing figures of Jesus, Buddha, or the deity they worshipped during their lifetime.

These emotionally comforting figures are the greeters at the porthole of light, as we pass into the after-life. They read our thoughts stored in our emotional and mental seed atoms and can assume the form each individual feels most comforted by and who can best alleviate their fears during this transitional phase of death. Although the figures that appear before us may not be God directly or even our loved ones, the spiritual helpers knowing our thoughts appear at that moment necessary to comfort us.7

As we spiritually advance, our soul has the potential to spend more time in the higher astral regions in the after-life. We can choose to relive the scenes of our just-ended life with our loved ones through our projected thoughts.8 The experiences, which made us most happy and brought joy to others, can be relived with each loved one, including our pets. We can even create an environment of imagination with our loved ones.

Dr. Harry Kenmore would advise individuals not to contact loved ones through spirit mediums, because this could be very dangerous. Sometimes, you are contacting a disincarnate entity coming through the medium, posing as your loved one. Mischievous spirits can cause harm, give false messages, and may try to possess you. Discarnate souls, trapped in the lower astral realm, have the capacity to read the thought forms of the recently departed loved one's etheric form. The etheric form always remains close to the corpse of the departed soul while it decomposes. Just after death, their thought forms are strong and can easily be intercepted by the disincarnate entities. Your loved one, in most cases, progresses beyond the lower astral realm to continue their after-life experience, and direct medium contact may not be possible.

Where does this link with our loved ones first originate? Each individual soul has entered evolution with a group of souls, or *"soul group"*. This soul group goes through the experiences of evolution and reincarnation together until the karmic ties are satisfied. When we reach the human stage, we begin to call this group our family and close circle of friends, although sometimes, because of specific karma, we may reincarnate outside of the family or *"soul group"* for singular life experiences.

The *"soul group"* or *"group karma"* we karmically incarnate with, referred to by Edgar Cayce, takes on different roles in our many lifetimes to fulfill the karmic needs of all the individual souls in the group.9 In one life, the soul you grow to love as a mother or father may die and reincarnate back into your family as your child or grandchild. Your spouse might have been someone close to you in a past life, other than a husband or wife. Individual souls with a very close bond are sometimes called *"soulmates."* Secondary soulmates might be referred to as *"karmic colleagues."* They are individual souls who, within our circle of influence, become our close and best friends.

We are always connected to our loved ones, as our individual soul journeys through the circle of life and death. Although our relationship with those we loved may not repeat itself in the same way when we were together on earth, over our many lifetimes, we will encounter the same souls over and over again. Whether we see our loved ones on earth, during sleep, in the astral realm, or in the after-life, we should take comfort in knowing that through karma and love we are always close.

Chapter Reflections to Guide Your Spiritual Search

- Your loved ones will always feel your thoughts of love, whether they are in the astral world or reincarnated back on earth in a physical body.

- When you think of your recently departed loved one before going to bed, you will most likely reunite with him or her during your sleep phase in the astral realm.

- We are drawn to our loved ones in the after-life spheres through our mutual vibrational level and love.

- *"Humanity understands but imperfectly the mysterious forces dwelling in the borderland between the living and the dead. Until man understands more, he should leave alone these forces which may only lead to madness."*[10]

References

1. Besant, Annie. *Death—And After?*, 84-85
2. Woodward, Mary Ann. *Edgar Cayce's Story of Karma*, 144-146
3. Baba, Meher. *Discourses*, 323-326
4. Woodward, Mary Ann. *Edgar Cayce's Story of Karma*, 251-252
5. Duce, Ivy O. *How a Master Works*, 637-638
6. Chaney, Earlyne. *The Mystery of Death and Dying*, 81-85
7. Moody, Raymond A. *Life After Life*, 58-64
8. Green, Harvey A. *Life and Death: The Pilgrimage of the Soul*, 93-113
9. Green, Harvey A. *Life and Death: The Pilgrimage of the Soul*, 93-94
10. Hall, Manly P. *Questions and Answers*, 95

    *McCreery, John. www.rosicrucians.com

20

Love and Soulmates

"In learning about the mystic Edgar Cayce, many had read that love at first sight, the instant feeling of familiarity with strangers, was a lingering remembrance from the dim past, with the promise of a love that passeth earthly understanding."

—*Jess Stearn* *

Love in one form or another is the binding attraction that propels creation forward in the progression of the soul through life and death. In the lower kingdoms of creation, the attraction of the opposite sex within species can be looked upon as a lesser degree of love when compared to human love. This attraction exists to perpetuate and move forward the experience of consciousness through physical forms as the soul journeys through evolution. Without this force of love, there would be no continuation of the species.1

Human love is this same attracting force functioning on a higher level. As the individual soul progresses to the highest level of love, the soul is drawn by God's Divine love to enter the spiritual path. This beginning of the individual soul's spiritual journey is termed involution (the soul searches inward). This love that propels us from within oneself to search for and experience God is called Divine Love.2

Throughout history, human consciousness progressed from instinct to reason with the dawning of the intellect. Presently, civilization is showing signs of the intellect awakening to intuition. In the same respect, the lower form of love in early human beings was the attraction to the opposite sex, where lust predominated. At each stage of humanity's development, love rises to a higher level. There is a difference between the attraction of lust and love. Each soul experiences the level of love, according to their evolutionary stage and spiritual development.

The soul in its true spiritual form in the after-life before each incarnation into a human body, has no sex differentiation. The latent impressions associated with a male or female gender will determine the orientation of the individual soul on earth. While in the physical form, the soul will seek equilibrium to balance the manifest impressions of either male or female. This force for balance, yin and yang, is the attraction between the sexes on earth. Human beings in a more civilized, evolving state of consciousness will psychically seek a sexual balance in a relationship of marriage with the opposite gender—a semi-symbolic completeness.

C. W. Leadbeater describes the difference between falling in love and love at first sight.

> *"This latter phenomenon (if it ever really occurs, as I am inclined to think it does) must mean the recognition by the ego of one who is well known in previous incarnations; but the former and more ordinary variety is usually due to the intensified action of repeated thought."*3

A repeated thought for someone of the opposite sex, due to an initial attraction, would be called falling in love. Leadbeater goes on to state that if you were exposed to one hundred people of the opposite sex, you could find reasons to fall in love with all of them, if allowed to. Today, relationships mainly begin with a physical attraction—how one smiles, facial features, their hair length and color, the shape of their body and movements. Eventually over time, true, inspired love may develop in the relationship. When love does not grow, individuals may begin to stray. They meet someone else and start to think about him or her. Affairs begin and marriages split. One could say there never really was true love between them to begin with.

In the case of soulmates, there is an immediate recognition by the individual souls from a previous incarnation. This recognition is usually instantaneous due to a previous karmic connection, whereby in a past lifetime there was a bonding of true love. It is the ego's recognition of love for another soul that is unconsciously experienced. This might be the meeting again of a loved one from a past incarnation that I related in the chapter "Seeing Our Loved Ones Again."

This instant recognition may also occur with pets. One might walk into a pet store or Humane League and see a dog, cat, or bird that one is suddenly drawn to without a clear reason. That animal's soul might have been one of your pets in a previous incarnation or a pet that you might have had as a child in your present incarnation. The soul of that animal also will seem to be drawn to you right away as if it was always in your care.4

Soulmates have a precious bond with one another. Their relationship in a previous lifetime would have been one of tenderness and love for each other. They might have even been brother and sister, best friends, or a parent and child in a past life. The relationship is not necessarily a repeat of lovers from another lifetime but a lifetime of love between two individual souls.

The key difference in the karmic relationship between soulmates and non-soulmates is the feeling between them that they always knew each other. In a relationship where the individual souls are karmically meeting each other for the first time, there is the excitement of finding out about one another. They may end the relationship quickly when the excitement of this new relationship is gone and their expectations of each other are not met.

Soulmates feel that they have always known and accepted each other. Their expectations are satisfied from the beginning of the relationship. They are in sync with one another; it is as if their two souls are one. Soulmates usually have very similar interests; their temperaments balance each other and maintain a rhythm in the relationship. One partner might have a tendency to spend money, the other uses restraint and a mutual beneficial outcome is achieved. They seem to act as one, many times thinking the same thoughts at the same moment. They feel a spiritual harmony together. Neither one would ever think of hurting the other. They spend their lives helping each other to grow spiritually and realize their common life's purpose. Many times their careers are interwoven.5

Souls begin to develop their soulmate connection early in the reincarnation process. When souls begin reincarnating with human consciousness they become part of a *"soul pool."* The souls are part of a cluster of souls that exist on the same vibrational level. They reincarnate with one another throughout time and space. As time goes on, the *"soul pool"* diminishes and associations are maintained only between the individuals where there is a strong bond of love.

You may find your soulmate at any time during your life. Many times, one finds their soul mate early in life only to be parted shortly after making the connection when one is taken away by illness or war. Soulmates who meet later in life may only remain together for a short period of time. A sixty-year-old widow may be drawn to her soulmate, lending support and care to each other in their advancing years.

There is the possibility that soulmates will not reincarnate together in each life. If you and your soulmate incarnate into the same time period and meet, you may not become husband or wife in this lifetime. He or she may reincarnate as your parent or sibling depending on the type of relationship that you both need to experience. Eventually, as one begins the path of involution, you will begin to search for your ultimate soulmate—God, The Creator of all souls, the only Soul to love and reunite with forever.

Chapter Reflections to Guide Your Spiritual Search

- Love in one form or another is the binding attraction that propels creation forward.

- Soulmates do not always appear in the beginning of one's life. There may be a great deal of age difference. There may also be a race and cultural differences.

- Let your intuition guide you in the recognition of your soulmate.

- Living with your soulmate creates a balanced, harmonious life.

- Soulmates help each other to grow spiritually. Your soulmate in life is your spiritual counterpart for that lifetime, and the relationship is spiritually beneficial to both of you.

References

1. Baba, Meher. *Discourses,* 400-402
2. Baba, Meher. *The Path of Love,* 53-56
3. Leadbeater, C.W. *The Hidden Side of Things,* 427
4. Green, Harvey A. *Life and Death: The Pilgrimage of the Soul,* 57
5. Stearn, Jess. *Soulmates,* 51-65

    *Stearn, Jess. *Soulmates,* 7

21

Preparing for Our Return

"Some things have been mastered, much more remains to
be accomplished and the soul is drawn irresistibly back to
the sphere of its unfinished labors."

—*Manly P. Hall* *

Now that our after-life experience in the other realms of reality is complete,
we are refreshed and renewed. The karma from our last earth life has been
reviewed and assimilated into our permanent unconsciousness, in the mental
body. With the assimilated earthly impressions as wisdom, we can return to
earth with a better inner sense of how to conduct ourselves in the next karmic
life-phase. We also experienced all that the after-life had to offer, according
to our vibrational and spiritual level. We are now prepared to plan, with our
guardian angel, for our return to the earthly plane—our next incarnation.

The lives of individual souls that have been cut short—either from an
early death due to an accident, murder, or suicide—usually wish to return
too quickly to earth again. Their desire to finish up their last life's purpose
and sanskaras cause them to rush through their after-life experience. This
impatience may be the result of dwelling in the lower astral plane, close to the

earth, until their destined karmic time was complete. But their impatience will cost them valuable preparation time in the after-life.1

There are also individual souls who squandered their lessons. They did not achieve a wholesome period of recovery or a complete ego-mind modification to enable them to make much progress during this new incarnation. In the astral realm, as on earth, you retain your free will. Although the teachers in this realm may suggest our path, we do not always pay attention to their advice and follow their guidance. However, most individual souls inwardly are aware that it is for their best good to accept their guardian angel's guidance.2

Timing of your return becomes a personal choice as you spiritually advance, but younger souls just entering the human stage of reincarnation may not be in a position to plan their next incarnation. Their after-death experience is different. For them the after-life becomes a deep sleep of unconsciousness. They need to gain experiences before they have anything to assimilate. As soon as four days later, their soul can be enlivening the body of a fetus in a mother's womb.3

These souls need to gain a certain amount of experience and knowledge on earth before they can be involved in after-life reflection and interaction with the higher spirits. Younger souls are at the whim of their evolutionary stage and their emotions, which through time and experience they learn to control through free will and gained wisdom. They need to live through many lifetimes, gathering experiences to have impressions of the opposites, enabling them to develop the intelligence for discrimination of their actions on earth. Until then, their time spent in the after-life is similar to a student in his early education years, accumulating the foundation of knowledge and wisdom.4

As Dolores Cannon explains, throughout our spiritual journey between earthly incarnations, we live and interact with souls from our families and communities. We are drawn together by the similarity of our vibrations and love within our subtle and mental bodies. Because of this affinity between the individuals of *"group souls,"* we will try to plan with them in the astral world for our return together. Life plans are developed, based on karmic considerations that can be met for the current time period. These choices are made in a similar way to how we plan on earth.

Step-by-step decisions for each aspect of this new life are made. At this time, we will be deciding in which country we will live, the community, religion, family, parents, and gender we will need to incarnate into. We may even choose our spouse, possibly our soulmate, for the upcoming life! The exact details do not come into play at this time. Instead, we have an awareness of the overall pattern of relationships and circumstances that lie before us.5

Harvey A. Green, in his book, *Life and Death: The Pilgrimage of the Soul*, focuses on two major factors that are considered in the rebirth planning phase—motivation and potential. Our motivation has to do with our purpose in each life. This is one force that keeps drawing us back to live another life on earth. To accomplish our purpose, we work within our potential. The personality, talents, intellect, and physical characteristics that we need are all part of our potential to work with our motivating forces. How we used our potential in our last incarnation, and the impact our choices had both positive and negative, are stored in our seed atoms as sanskaric memories influencing our choices for the next earthly adventure.

Karma bridges motivation and potential, which keeps us afloat in materiality to achieve our goals. As we cannot possibly meet every karmic relationship at once, the time we spend planning for each aspect becomes our karma only for the upcoming life. Certain periods of time on earth are more beneficial than others, as well as the availability for specific parents. If we need to develop a certain talent, we will need the right genetic make up for the best expression of that talent. A singer needs the necessary vocal cords, the pianist the specific type of hand formation, and the scientist requires a highly developed cognitive brain capacity.

> *When the proximity is correct, when conditions are best, we then make a final decision and in so doing we gain immeasurably. Half the gain in life is "showing up"; consequently, according to Edgar Cayce, half the gain in an earthly incarnation is in deciding to do it. Throughout the whole of the experience the angels of grace are there to give us all that we have need of at any time. They are likewise ever present to help us in our decisions regarding our next material incarnation.6*

The individual soul usually watches over the parents he or she has chosen for rebirth, to see if they will fit the requirements for the planned life's karma. As the time for rebirth grows near, the soul moves closer and closer to see the potential for this incarnation more clearly. The material realm comes closer into view. Helpers are still there to bridge the gap between the earth and the astral plane. The soul is now ready to go from the spirit realm to the material realm. It is the sum total of the karmic choices that propel the individual soul into the material realm and out of the spirit world. The consciousness slowly loses its place for now in the spirit world as it merges into contact with the physical brain of the developing infant.7

From the spirit world, the individual soul can usually observe the formation of their developing physical body in the mother's womb. The soul may enter the womb at any time, if the soul wishes to experience itself within the growing fetus and the birth process. 8 This experience may not be advisable because the soul is subjected to the mother's fluctuating emotions, which may be disturbing.

Religious scholars and theologians continue to debate when the soul enters the newly forming physical body and life begins. There is a vast difference between spiritual beliefs on this topic, ranging from *"life only begins at conception"* to the entrance of the individual soul which may take place any time after conception.9,10 Edgar Cayce stated that he believed the soul may enter the physical body when the first breath of life is drawn.11

If the soul experiences negative emotions about the upcoming birth, the soul may try to leave the womb and sever the connection with the developing fetus. If the soul is successful, the result will be a miscarriage or stillbirth without any karmic consequences. The guardian angels do their best to assist each soul during this important phase of birth. However, each individual soul still has free will, (within their sanskaric pool), to make their own decisions.

Preparing for our return to earth is an important transitional phase between death and life. The impressions from the last incarnation have now been assimilated into the memory-seed atoms during this after-life experience and the karma for the upcoming life has been determined. How we cared for our physical body in the previous life, whether we took care of it or mistreated it, will also contribute to the condition of the new incarnating physical form. All interactions in the spirit realm with the higher evolved souls also contributed to the growth of our inner spiritual wisdom and intuition, which will guide our soul in making the appropriate choices for our next life on earth. Until we become consciously awakened to the experience of God within, the circle of life and death will continue.

Chapter Reflections to Guide Your Spiritual Search

- While in the astral world, assimilate as much as you can, so you can return to earth with greater wisdom and spiritual growth.

- We are drawn to our families and communities by the similarity of our vibrations and love within our subtle and mental bodies.

- Expecting mothers should be extremely careful with their emotions and thoughts. The individual soul may be vitalizing the physical form at any-time in your pregnancy. You want the entering soul to feel comfortable and happy in this environment.

- Follow the advice of your guardian angels while you prepare to reincarnate. They can see the bigger spiritual picture in your soul's evolutionary journey.

References

1. Green, Harvey A. *Life and Death: The Pilgrimage of the Soul*, 115-116
2. Cannon, Dolores. *Between Death and Life*, 179-186
3. Baba, Meher. Ed. Don E. Stevens. *Listen Humanity*, 104-105
4. Cannon, Dolores. *Between Death and Life*, 35-61
5. Baba, Meher. *Discourses*, 319-322
6. Green, Harvey A. *Life and Death: The Pilgrimage of the Soul*, 119
7. Green, Harvey A. *Life and Death: The Pilgrimage of the Soul*, 122
8. Cannon, Dolores. *Between Death and Life*, 228-234
9. Heindel, Max. *The Rosicrucian Christianity Lectures*, 138-139
10. Kaplan, Pascal. *Understanding Death from a Spiritual Perspective*, 37.
11. Woodward, Mary Ann. *Edgar Cayce's Story of Karma*, 252-253

*Hall, Manly P. *Questions and Answers*, 93

Afterward

Now that your introduction to the spiritual progression of the individual soul journeying through the circle of life and death is complete you can breathe a sigh of relief. You have taken an important step as a spiritual seeker. This journey is strewn with obstacles and challenges, as well as joys and pleasures. I hope this book will guide you to experience a happier life and better death experience as you awaken your spiritual potential and develop your relationship with God, your *"constant companion"*.

As you strive to find your purpose in each lifetime, the knowledge and practical strategies you have gained should provide you with inspiration to use your spiritual intuition, and seek your highest aspirations. This understanding and knowledge of your Divine Ancestry and the scheme of the Universal Laws at work in your life and the universe will never be lost as you progress lifetime after lifetime.

The teachings presented in this book assure us that the soul will always continue after each physical death: it is immortal. The physical body is only a cover and changes with each incarnation. Although we must all leave our loved ones and familiar surroundings after each life we live, we can take hope that we will meet those we loved again in the after-life or on earth in another incarnation.

Through our lessons and experiences, we awaken wisdom and truth until we return to our ancient heritage of one with God, which answers the question, Who am I? But we must go through countless lifetimes before we can return home. I wish you all well as a fellow seeker on this journey.

Ghazal

This world exists; but is not your final abode.
Turn your face toward God.
How long will you live in this transient world?
It is a testing ground of virtue and vice for you to experience.

Slacken not your effort in worshiping God;
look upon every breath as your last.
You know not what will happen tomorrow;
so be prepared today for the future.

Conditions in the world have not changed
but marvelous have been the visitors to this world.
From the garden of this world have departed
millions of beings like nightingales;
hundreds of thousands more will come and go.

Atma, the Soul, is one; varied are the bodies indeed
like the many sons of one Father cherished.
Behold there, on the meadow of love,
many a rider of varigated colors flourishes.

Without adversity there is no rest.
In hardship and sorrow be grateful and at peace.
In distress, always keep content;
have patience, and at all times be at ease.

Continuously washing your clothes is a waste of time;
instead, purify your heart with the thought of God divine.
Behold, at the feet of one God in form,
every moment hundreds of souls lie in sacrifice.

Do not take forbidden intoxicants;
better to live a life of honor and esteem.
Learn to live in the unique intoxication
of the early morning love of God.

God is matchless, one in all! See Him in your heart.
See Him also as the God manifest, the God concealed,
the God within you and the God without.

Man, in your boast you lost the status of an angel,
pride has reduced you to a devil.
Oh Huma, in this world of passing show,
behold, like you, such innumerable players come and go.

*Huma– Meher Baba's pen name in the 1920's

Kalchuri, Bhau. *Lord Meher.* vol. 2, 417

Glossary

Akashic records: A storehouse containing the records of every deed, word, thought, feeling, action, and event of every soul since the dawn of each soul's existence. This is also referred to as the Book of Life or the Book of Judgement.

Astral body: The newly formed spirit vehicle that the subtle and mental spirit bodies use to enter and experience the astral plane in the after-life.

Astral plane: The world closest to our physical world which souls enter when leaving their physical form upon death. It is a world normally invisible to the five senses.

Astral travel: The soul's ability, during sleep, to leave the physical form with the mental and subtle (emotional) spirit bodies and travel into the astral world.

Aura: An emanation of a colored cloud of light surrounding the physical body as a reflection of vibrations of the soul.

Avatar: The Messiah, Christ, God in human form or God-Man.

Chi: The Universal life force.

Clear Light of the Void: This is the Light of God in the true state of infinite bliss devoid of all limitations and darkness.

Disincarnate entity: Souls inhabiting the astral plane unable to progress forward in the after-life. Such trapped souls are usually victims of murder, accident, and suicide.

Ego-mind: The intergrating nucleus of consciousness that allows our impressions to express themselves rationally.

Emotional seed atom: The emotional seed atom holds the record of all the qualities of your emotional weaknesses and strengths gathered throughout your soul's evolutionary lives. This atom is in our subtle body of the spirit in the proximity of the solar plexus of the physical body.

Epoch: A cycle or period of time in terms of noteworthy events.

Esoteric: The secret teachings of all religions and philosophies shared with the chosen few.

Ghazal: The Ghazal is an ancient Persian form of poetry.

God: God is. God is everything and everyone, consciously and unconsciously. The manifest creation is but a shadow of God's Reality.

Hafiz: Shamsuddin Muhammad Hafiz was a 14th century Perfect Master and poet of Shiraz. He died in 1389 A.D.

Heart seed atom: This atom is situated in the area of the heart. It is a visual recording of your entire evolutionary past karmic information. It contains every thought, physical characteristic, emotion, and action from your past while it continues to record all aspects in your present life.

Hierarchy: The spiritual body governing all manifest creation. There are 56 God Realized Souls on earth at all times. Five of these 56 souls are always Perfect Masters. Every seven to fourteen hundred years, the Messiah or God-Man descends to earth to assume His position at the head of the hierarchy to set the pattern guiding creation until the next advent.

Involution: When the consciousness of the individual soul begins to turn inward towards God.

Kali Yuga: A cycle of time in an epoch, lasting 26,000 years according to the Hindu system. There are four ages within a Yuga. Each age corresponds to birth, growth, maturity, and decay. Kali is the age of decay. We are currently 5,000 years into the Kali Yuga or Dark Age.

Matrix: The laying of the foundation for the development of the growing physical fetus in the mothers womb.

Mental seed atom: The mental seed atom interpenetrates the pineal gland in your brain, through the mental body. This atom holds the record of all your mental thoughts from the beginning of your soul's human evolutionary journey.

Mukti: Liberation from the circle of life and death. Continuous experience of the God state of bliss.

Nirvana: The Buddhist belief of the heavenly state attained by the pure soul. Freedom from the cycle of births and deaths.

No-Eyes: A blind, psychic, Chippewa medicine woman who guided Mary Summer Rain through mystical journeys of the world's future.

Perfection: The soul's conscious attainment of all power, knowledge, and bliss—God Realization.

Perfect Master: A Perfect Master is one who has become God realized, (after completing the journey of evolution, reincarnation, and involution). He or she functions in the physical world, overseeing the events on earth, but has consciousness of the subtle and mental worlds, while maintaining his or her God-conscious state. There are always five Perfect Masters on earth at all times. When one drops his/her physical form, another is ready to take his/her place. John the Baptist was considered one of the five Perfect Masters alive during the time of Jesus Christ. 3

Phoenix Days: The Phoenix is an ancient, Egyptian, mythological bird symbolic of eternal life: rebirth, renewal of life and resurrection of truth.

Prana: The vital life force.

Psyche: The ego-mind functions out of the psyche.

Sanskara: Sanskaras (impressions) are created from earthly experiences and stored in the seed atoms of the subtle and mental bodies of the soul. These old sanskaric impressions come with us to each earth incarnation to be expended. In the process of expending them, we create new sanskaras.

Silver Cord: The Silver Cord unites the higher vehicles (subtle and mental bodies) to the lower vehicles of the soul (etheric and physical bodies). This cord snaps when death occurs.

Soul personality: The intergrated sum total of the soul's personalities through reincarnation and involution.

Spiritual intuition: Infinite knowledge of spiritual values and the inner life is unveiled to each individual soul as intuition. Intuition is the first stage of spiritual life, which can be awakened through the practice of prayer, meditation and self-less service.

Vibration: Everything in the universe is a complex of vibratory rates. Music, color, thoughts, and even human cells vibrate at different rates. When we are capable of refining our mental and emotional vibrations we will be able master the mystery of life and death.

Resources

Avatar Meher Baba Trust
Kings Road, Post Bag 31
Ahmednagar 414 0011
MS India
Phone: (+91) 241-2342666
www.ambppct.org

Astara
792 West Arrow Highway
P.O. Box 5003
Upland, California 91785-5003
Phone: 909-981-4941
www.astara.org

Edgar Cayce's Association for Research and Enlightenment, Inc. (A.R.E.)
215 67th Street
Virginia Beach, Virginia 23451
Phone: 757-428-3588
www.edgarcayce.org

Inner Traditions Bear & Company
1 Park Street
Rochester, Vermont 05767
www.InnerTraditions.com

The International Headquarters of the Sufi Movement
24 Banstraat
2517 GJDen Haag
Netherlands
www.sufimovement.org

Meher Spiritual Center
10200 North Kings Highway
Myrtle Beach, South Carolina 29572
Phone: 843-272-5777
www.mehercenter.org

Meher Abode Australia Information
19 Meher Road
Woombye, Qld 4559
Australia
Phone: 61 (07) 54422 1544
www.avatarsabodee.com.au/

Ozark Mountain Publishing, Inc.
P.O. Box 754
Huntsville, Arkansas 72740
Phone: 479-7388-2348
www.ozarkmt.com

The Philosophical Research Society
3910 Los Feliz Boulevard
Los Angeles, California 90027
Phone: 323-663-2167
www.prs.org

The Rosicrucian Fellowship
2222 Mission Avenue
Oceanside, California 920544-2399
www.rosicrucianfellowship.org

Sheriar Foundation Bookstore
807 34th Avenue South
North Myrtle Beach, South Carolina 29582
Phone: 843-272-1339
www.sheriarbook.org

Sufism Reoriented
1300 Boulevard Way
Walnut Creek, California 94595
Searchlight Books
Phone: 925-934-9365
www.slbooks.com

The Theosophical Society in America
1926 North Main Street
Wheaton, Illinois 60189—0270
Phone: 630-665-0130
www.questbooks.net

The Theosophical Publishing House
Adyar, Chennai 6000 020
India
www.ts-adyar.org

Bibliography

Alder, Vera Stanley. *The Finding of the Third Eye.* London: Rider, 1937.

Arnold, Sir Edwin. *The Light of Asia.* Philadelphia: David McKay.

Avila, St. Teresa of. *Interior Castles.* Ed. E. Allison Peers. New York: Doubleday, 1989.

Baba, Meher. *Beams.* Walnut Creek, California: Sufism Reoriented, 1958

Baba, Meher. *Discourses.* 3 vols. San Francisco, California: Sufism Reoriented, 1968

Baba, Meher. *Discourses.* Myrtle Beach, South Carolina: Sheriar Press, 1987.

Baba, Meher. Ed. Don Stevens. *Listen Humanity.* New York: Dodd, Mead and Company, 1967

Baba, Meher. *Meher Baba on Inner Life.* Poona India: Meher Era Publications,1977.

Baba, Meher. *Meher Baba on War.* Poona India: Meher Era Publications, 1972.

Baba, Meher. *The Advancing Stream of Life.* Poona, India: Meher Era Publications, 1974.

Baba, Meher. *The Path of Love.* New York: Samuel Weiser, 1976

Baba, Meher. *The Secret of Sleep.* Poona, India: Meher Era Publication, 1968.

Besant, Annie. *Death and After.* Madras, India: Theosophical Publishing House, 1991.

Besant, Annie. *Karma.* Madras, India: Theosophical Publishing House, 1986

Besant, Annie. *Man and His Bodies.* Madras, India: The Theosophical Publishing House, 1990.

Besant, Annie. *Reincarnation.* Madras, India: Theosophical Publishing House, 1994.

Besant, Annie. *The Riddle of Life.* Wheaton, Illinois: Theosophical Publishing House, 1994.

Bhagavad-Gita. Trans. Sir Edwin Arnold. London: Routledge and Kegan Paul , 1948.

Brinkley, Dannion and Paul Perry. *Saved by the Light.* New York: Villard Books, 1994.

Bro, Harmon H., Ph.D. *Edgar Cayce on Dreams*. New York: Warner Books, 1988.

Bro, Harmon H., Ph.D. *Edgar Cayce on Religion and Psychic Experience*. Ed. Hugh Lynn Cayce. New York: Warner Books, 1988.

Burns, David D., M.D. *Feeling Good—The New Mood Therapy*. New York: Nal Penguin, 1980.

Buscaglia, Leo, Ph.D. *Living, Loving and Learning*. New York: Ballantine Books, 1983.

Bynner, Witter. *The Way of Life According to Laotzu*. New York: John Day, 1944.

Byock, Ira, M.D. *Dying Well-The Prospect for Growth at the End of Life*. New York: Riverhead Books, 1997.

Caldwell, Taylor. *The Romance of Atlantis*. Connecticut: Fawcett Crest Book, 1975.

Cannon, Alexander, Dr. *The Power of Karma*. Paternoster Row, England: Rider.

Cannon, Dolores. *Between Death and Life*. Huntsville, Arkansas: Ozark Mountain Publishers, 1995.

Carlson, Richard, Ph.D. *Don't Sweat The Small Stuff...and It's All Small Stuff*. New York: Hyperion, 1997.

Carrel, Alexis, Dr. *Prayer*. New York: Morehouse-Gorham, 1948.

Cayce, Edgar. *Auras*. Virginia Beach, Virginia: A.R.E. Press, 1996.

Cayce, Edgar. *Individual Reference File-Extracts from the Edgar Cayce Readings*. Virginia Beach, Virginia: A.R.E. Press, 1976.

Cerminara, Gina. *Many Mansions*. New York: Signet Book, 1978.

Cerminara, Gina. *The World Within*. New York: William Sloane Associates, 1957.

Chadwick, Gloria. *Discovering Your Past Lives*. Chicago, Illinois: Contemporary Books, 1988.

Chaney, Earlyne. *The Mystery of Death and Dying*. York Beach, Maine: Samuel Weiser, 1989.

Church, W. H. *Edgar Cayce's Story of the Soul*. Virginia Beach, Virginia: A.R.E. Press, 1993.

Collier, Robert. *The Book of Life*. 7 vols. New York: Robert Collier, 1925.

Conybeare, Irene. *Civilisation or Chaos?* Bombay, India: Popular Press, 1959.

Cotter, Patrick. *How to Pray*. Boca Raton, Florida: Globe Communications, 1997.

Dickens, Charles. *A Christmas Carol*. New York: Bantam Books, 1986.

Doyle, Sir Arthur Conan. *The Complete Novel and Stories*. vol. 11. New York: Bantam Books, 1945.

Duce, Ivy Oneita. *How a Master Works*. Walnut Creek, California: Sufism

Reoriented, 1975.

Duce, Ivy Oneita. *What Am I Doing Here?* Walnut Creek, California: Sufism Reoriented, 1976.

Emerson, Ralph Waldo. *The Complete Writings of Ralph Waldo Emerson.* New York: William H. Wise, 1929.

Fox, Emmet. *Reincarnation-Described and Explained.* New York: Harper and Brothers, 1939.

Gaer, Joseph. *How the Great Religions Began.* New York: New American Library, 1955.

Gibran, Kahlil. *The Kahlil Gibran Reader- Inspirational Writings.* New York: Kensington Publishing, 1976.

Gibran, Kahlil. *The Prophet.* New York: Alfred A. Knopf, 1968.

Gawain, Shakti. *Creative Visualization.* New York: Bantam Books, 1985.

Great Religions of the World. Ed. Robert McAfee Brown, Amiya Chakravarty et al. Washington D.C.: National Geographic Society, 1971

Green, Arthur Jay. *The Science of the Mind.* U.S.A.: The American Federation of Truth, 1939.

Green, Harvey. *Life and Death: The Pilgrimage of the Soul.* Virginia Beach, Virginia: A.R.E. Press, 1998.

Gumpert, Martin, MD. *The Anatomy of Happiness.* New York: McGraw-Hill Book, 1951.

Hall, Edward T. *The Hidden Dimension.* Garden City, New York: Doubleday, 1969.

Hall, Manly Palmer. *The Adepts-In the Eastern Esoteric Tradition.* Part 5. Los Angeles, California: The Philosophical Research Society, 1988.

Hall, Manly Palmer, *A Commentary Upon the Quiet Way.* Los Angeles, California: The Philosophical Research Society, Inc., 1955.

Hall, Manly Palmer. *Death to Rebirth.* Los Angeles, California: Philosophical Research Society, 1979.

Hall, Manly Palmer. *How Belief in Rebirth Enriches Your Life.* Los Angeles, California: Philosophical Research Society, 1956.

Hall, Manly Palmer. *Invisible Records of Thought and Action.* Los Angeles, California: Philosophical Research Society, 1990.

Hall, Manly Palmer. *Pathways of Philosophy.* Los Angeles, California: Philosophical Research Society, 1947.

Hall, Manly Palmer. *Questions and Answers.* Los Angeles, California: Philosophical Research Society, 1965.

Hall, Manly Palmer. *Reincarnation: The Cycle of Necessity.* Los Angeles, California: Philosophical Research Society, 1956.

Hall, Manly Palmer. *The Value of Prayer in Psychological Integration.* Los Angeles, California: Philosophical Research Society, 1955.

Heindel, Max. *Occult Principles of Health and Healing.* Oceanside, California: Rosicrucian Fellowship, 1938.

Heindel, Max. *The Rosicrucian Christianity Lectures.* Oceanside, California: Rosicrucian Fellowship, 1985.

Heindel, Max. *The Web of Destiny.* Oceanside, California: Rosicrucian Fellowship, 1928.

Judge, William Q. *The Ocean of Theosophy.* Point Loma, California: Theosophical University Press.

Jung, Carl Gustav. *Psychology and the East.* Princeton, New Jersey: Princeton University Press, 1990.

Jung, Carl Gustav. *Psychology and Religion.* New Haven: Yale University Press, 1947.

Kalchuri, Bhau. *Avatar of the Age Meher Baba Manifesting.* North Myrtle Beach, South Carolina: MANifestation, 1985.

Kalchuri, Bhau. *The Nothing and The Everything.* North Myrtle Beach, South Carolina: MANifestation, 1981.

Kalchuri, Bhau. *Lord Meher.* 20 vols. Ashville, North Carolina: MANifestation, 2001.

Kaplan, Pascal M.,Ph.D. *Understanding Death from a Spiritual Perspective.* Walnut Creek, California: Sufism Reoriented, 1977.

Kennedy, Maud. *The Immortal Hafiz.* North Myrtle Beach, South Carolina: MANifestation, 1987.

Khan, Inayat. *The Awakening of the Human Spirit.* New Lebanon, New York: Omega Press, 1988.

Khan, Inayat. *The Development of Spiritual Healing.* Claremont, California: Hunter House, Inc., Publishers, 1988.

Khan, Inayat. *The Inner Life.* London: Luzacc and Company, 1936.

Khan, Inayat. *Mastery Through Accomplishment.* New Lebanon, New York: Omega Press, 1989.

Khan, Inayat. *The Purpose of Life.* London: The Sufi Movement, 1927.

Khan, Inayat. *The Palace of Mirrors.* Great Britain: Sufi Publishing, 1976.

Khan, Inayat. *Spiritual Dimensions of Psychology.* New Lebanon, New York: Omega Press, 1988.

Khan, Inayat. *The Sufi Message of Inayat Khan-The Art of Personality.* Geneva: International Headquarters of Sufi Movement, 1982.

Khan, Inayat. *"The Soul, Whence and Whither?", The Sufi Message of Inayat Khan.* London: Barrie and Rockliff, 1960.

Khan, Inayat. *Yesterday, To-day and To-morrow.* London: Luzacc, 1935.

Khan, Inyat. *Education.* London: Luzacc, 1934.

Kowalski, Gary. *The Souls of Animals.* Walpole, New Hampshire: Stillpoint, 1991.

Lama, Dalai HH and Howard C. Cutler, MD. *The Art of Happiness—A Handbook for Living.* Great Britain: Hodder and Stoughton, 1999.

Langley, Noel. *Edgar Cayce on Reincarnation.* New York: Castle Books, 1967.

Leadbeater, C.W. *The Astral Plane.* Madras, India: Theosophical Publishing House, 1987.

Leadbeater, C.W. *Dreams.* Madras, India: Theosophical Publishing House, 1984.

Leadbeater, C.W. *Invisible Helpers.* Madras, India: Theosophical Publishing House, 1994.

Leadbeater, C. W. *The Life and After.* Madras, India: Theosophical Publishing House, 1994.

Leadbeater, C.W. *The Hidden Side of Things.* Madras, India: Theosophical Publishing House, 1948.

Leadbeater, C.W. *The Inner Life.* Chicago, Illinois: Rajput Press, 1911.

Leadbeater, C.W. *The Masters and the Path.* Madras, India: Theosophical Publishing House, 1969.

Lewis, H. Spencer. *Mansions of the Soul-The Cosmic Conception.* San Jose, California: Rosicrucian Press, 1967.

Lewis, H. Spencer. *A Thousand Years of Yesterdays.* San Jose, California: Rosicrucian Press, 1945.

Maharaja, Sadguru Upasani-Baba. *The Talks of Sadguru Upasani-Baba Maharaja.* 4 vols. Nagpur, India: Dr. Sahasrabudhe, 1976

Montagu, Ashley. *Life before Birth.* New York: New American Library of World Literature, 1964.

Montgomery, Ruth. *Here and Hereafter.* New York: Fawcett Crest, 1991.

Montgomery, Ruth. *The World Before.* New York: Ballantine Books, 1990.

Montgomery, Ruth. *A World Beyond.* New York: Coward, McCann and Geoghegan, 1971.

Moody, Raymond A., JR., M.D. *Life After Life.* New York: Bantam Books, 1976.

Mulford, Prentice. *Thought Forces.* London: G. Bell and Sons, 1913.

Peale, Norman Vincent. *The New Art of Living.* New York: Ballantine Books, 1989.

Peale, Norman Vincent. *The Power of Positive Thinking.* New York: Ballantine Books, 1990.

Peale, Norman Vincent. *Expect a Miracle-Make Miracles Happen.* Carmel, New York: Guideposts, 1974.

Peck, M. Scott, M.D. *Further Along the Road less Traveled.* New York: Simon and Schuster, 1993.

Peck, M. Scott, M.D. *The Road less Traveled.* New York: Phoenix Press,1985.

Ponder, Catherine. *The Dynamic Laws of Prayer.* Marina Del Rey, California: DeVorss and Company, 1987.

Rain, Mary Summer. *Phoenix Rising.* Norfolk, Virginia: Hampton Roads Publishing Company, 1993.

Robinson, Lytle. *Edgar Cayce's Story of The Origin and Destiny of Man.* New York: Coward, McCann and Geoghegan, 1976.

Sambhava, Padma. *The Tibetan Book of the Dead.* Trans. Thurman, Robert A.F. New York: Bantam Books, 1994.

Sanders, C.W. *The Inner Voice.* London: J.H.G.Wood, 1948.

Selections from the Rubaiyat and Odes of Hafiz. Ed. A Member of the Persia Society of London. London: John M. Watkins, 1920.

Siegel, Bernie S.,M.D. *Love, Medicine and Miracles.* New York: Harper and Row, 1986.

Shepherd, A.P. *A Scientist of the Invisible-An Introduction to the Life and Work of Rudolf Steiner.* New York: British Book Centre, 1959.

Smith, Huston. *The World's Religion: Our Great Wisdom Traditions.* San Francisco, California: Harper SanFrancisco, 1991.

Smith, A. Robert. *The Lost Memoirs of Edgar Cayce.* Virginia Beach, Virginia: A.R.E. Press, 1997.

Spence, Lewis. *Encyclopedia of Occultism.* New Hyde Park, New York: University Press, 1960.

Stearn, Jess. *Intimates Through Time-Edgar Cayce's Mysteries of Reincarnation.* New York: The Penguin Group, 1993.

Stearn, Jess. *Edgar Cayce-The Sleeping Prophet.* New York: Bantam Books, 1968.

Stearn, Jess. *The Search for a Soul-Taylor Caldwell's Psychic Lives.* Greenwich, Connecticut: Fawcett Publications, 1974.

Stearn, Jess. *Soulmates.* New York: Bantam Books, 1985.

Steiner, Rudolf. *The Influence of Spiritual Beings Upon Man.* Spring Valley, New York: Anthroposophic Press, 1982.

Steiner, Rudolf. *Karma.* New York: Anthroposophic Press, 1943.

Steiner, Rudolf. *Knowledge of the Higher Worlds and its Attainment.* New York: Anthroposophic Press, Inc., 1984.

Steiner, Rudolf, Ph.D. *Nutrition and Health.* Spring Valley, New York: Anthroposophic Press, Inc., 1987.

Steiner, Rudolf, Ph.D. *The Occult Significance of Blood.* London: Theosophical Publishing Society, 1912.

Steiner, Rudolf, Ph.D. *Reincarnation and Immortality.* New York: Multimedia, 1974.

Sugrue, Thomas, *There Is A River: The Story of Edgar Cayce.* New York: Henry Holt, 1948.

Sylvia, Claire with William Novak. *A Change of Heart.* New York: Little Brown.

Todeschi, Kevin J., M.A. *Edgar Cayce on the Akashic Records.* Virginia Beach, Virginia: A.R.E. Press, 1998.

Todeschi, Kevin J., M.A. *Edgar Cayce on the Reincarnation of Famous People.* Virginia Beach, Virginia: A.R.E. Press, 1998.

Thurston, Mark, Ph.D. *More Great Teachings of Edgar Cayce.* Virginia Beach, Virginia: A.R.E. Press, 1997

Wilkinson, Roy. *Rudolf Steiner on Education-A Compendium.* United Kingdom: Hawthorn Press, 1993.

Woodward, Mary Ann. *Edgar Cayce's Story of Karma.* New York: Berkley Publishing Group, 1972.

Zakaria, Rafiq. *Discovery of God.* Mumbai, India: Popular Prakashan, 2000.

Copyright Permissions

About the Author

Since the age of seventeen, Lawrence Karrasch wondered, what happens to us when we die? He has made it his life's passion to discover the answers to life and death questions, which he could not find through traditional religions. *The Circle of Life and Death* is a culmination of painstaking, investigative work, over many years, drawing from a broad range of esoteric and religious teachings on life, death and rebirth, from twentieth-century metaphysical writers to the prominent mystics and spiritual leaders of the modern era. To further this spiritual quest, he traveled to India over twenty times exploring eastern philosophy. As an art director in New York City, for most of his professional career, with a Master's degree from The Illinois Institute of Technology, he continues to pursue his spiritual path in his everyday life. He now resides with his wife, Rita, in Myrtle Beach, SC.

Printed in the United States
141685LV00003B/12/P